AF266347

The
Concept Of
LYING

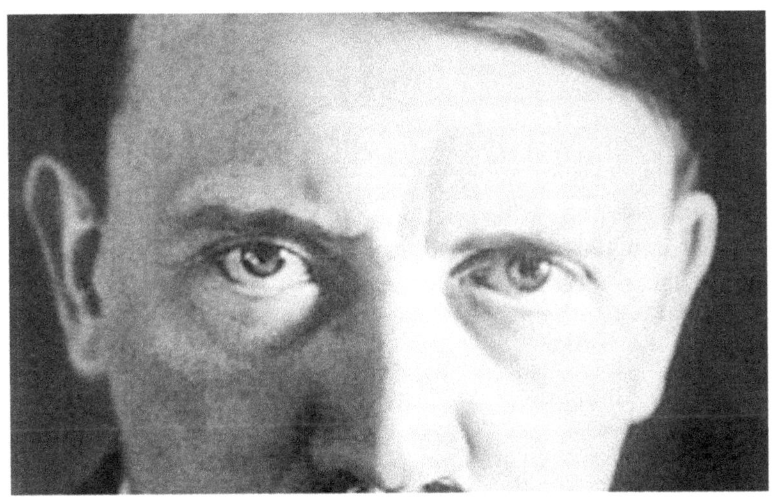

The

BIG Lie

Mike Kostelny, Ph.D.

Library of Congress Control Number: 2022911960

PAPERBACK: 978-1-957575-72-8
EBOOK: 978-1-957575-73-5

Ordering Information:

For orders and inquiries, please contact:
1-888-404-1388
www.goldtouchpress.com
book.orders@goldtouchpress.com

Printed in the United States of America

Nota Bene: Limit of Liability Notice

The Publisher and the Author make no representations with respect to the accuracy or completeness of the contents of this book. The strategies and advice contained herein may not be best suited for every situation. This book is SOLD with the understanding that the Publisher is not engaged in rendering, counselling, legal, or other professional services. Neither the Publisher, nor the Author, shall be liable for damages arising therefrom.

The fact that an Organization or Website or U-Tube Reference is referred to in this book as a citation and/or potential source of further information does not mean that the Author or the Publisher endorses the information the Organization or Website or U-Tube Reference may provide or recommendations it may make.

Readers should be made aware, furthermore, that internet websites and/or U-Tube References listed in this book may have changed (or disappeared altogether!) between the time this book was written (and published) and the time this book is read.

Thank you for your understanding.

Dedicatory Quote

Now, let me ask you something: what can one expect from man, considering he's such a strange creature? You can shower upon him all earthly blessings, drown him in happiness so that there'll be nothing to be seen but the bubbles rising to the surface of his bliss, give him such economic security that he won't have anything to do but sleep, nibble at cakes, and worry about keeping world history flowing—and even then, out of sheer spite and ingratitude, man will play a dirty trick on you.

He'll even risk his cake for the sake of the most glaring stupidity, for the most economically unsound nonsense, just to inject into all the soundness and sense surrounding him some of his own disastrous, lethal fancies. What he wants to preserve is precisely his noxious fancies and vulgar trivialities, if only to assure himself that men are still men (as if that were so important) and not piano keys simply responding to the laws of nature.

Man is somehow averse to the idea of being unable to desire unless this desire happens to figure on his timetable at that moment. But even if man was nothing but a piano key, even if this could be demonstrated to him mathematically—even then, he wouldn't come to his senses but would pull some trick out of sheer ingratitude, just to make his point. And if he didn't have them on hand, he would devise the means of destruction, chaos, and all kinds of suffering to get his way.

For instance, he'd swear loud enough for the whole world to hear—swearing is man's prerogative, setting him apart from the other animals—and maybe his swearing alone would get him what he wanted, that is, it'd prove to him that he's a man and not a piano key.

Now you may say that this too can be calculated in advance and entered on the timetable—chaos, swearing, and all—and that the very possibility of such a calculation would prevent it, so that sanity would prevail. Oh no! In that case man would go insane on purpose, just to be immune from reason.

I believe this is so and I'm prepared to vouch for it, because it seems to me that the meaning of man's life consists in proving to himself every minute that he's a man and not a piano key. And man will keep proving it and paying for it with his own skin; he will turn into a troglodyte if need be.

And, since this is so, I cannot help rejoicing that things are still the way they are and that, for the time being, nobody knows worth a damn what determines our desires.

—Fyodor Dostoevsky, *Notes from Underground*

Acknowledgements

As this work concerns 'The Concept of Lying,' I would be remiss if I did not thank the many people in my sphere of influence during my formative childhood years who have helped me to remember that "Honesty is always the Best Policy"! These people include teachers in my public-school years, as well as professors in Secondary and Tertiary Education throughout several schools, Colleges, and Universities, I attended.

I am also beholden to the fine military officers who helped instill in me a sense of duty and discipline during my four summers of militia training. Above all else, there is the example of The Christian Religion with its emphasis in defining "What Is Truth?", as well as my personal family, Church family, friends, and colleagues at work.

If I am to name names, I must include my mother, Lillian, who has been an example par excellence of the woman who never gives up believing in her son. Her simple faith has helped me to remain honest and truthful throughout the days of my life.

I am reminded of the following poem (by Margaret Scoutton; 1903-2001) that captures my mother's faith, entitled: "For Honor of Her!", which I quote in part (under Fair Use):

> Somewhere, a woman thrusting fear away,
> Faces the future bravely for your sake,
> Toils on from dawn till dusk, from day to day,

Fights back her tears, nor heeds the bitter ache.

She loves you, trusts you, breathes in prayer your
name;
Soil not her faith in you, by sin or shame;
Oh, keep for her dear sake, a stainless name;
Bring back to her a manhood free from shame.

And of course, there is my fiancée, Victoria, who remains
in East Ukraine (at the time of this writing) trying to help
her family there as best as she can. Her daily example of
raw courage, and unflinching loyalty both to me and the
rest of our family there (in the midst of rampant Fake News
and Russian propaganda) constantly reminds me why this
book must be written.

Notes of Explanation

This work (to entail an exposé on the unfair and, arguably, untrue tale told of the events and details leading up to Miss Monroe's passing) is not a definitive project. To be 100% accurate and convincing, it must have access to all the currently withheld secret files and classified information of that last weekend of Marilyn Monroe's life (from 03rd August to 06th August 1962).

Whether the Author's conclusion after reviewing updated material(s) may prove convincing to the reader (although desired) is not the main thrust of that exposé!

What I am hoping (and praying) is that my current research will be taken up by more able hands and more supple minds in these next few years to ensure that in 2039 (the year promised to release all these heretofore 'hidden' documents) the Truth will prevail.

I trust and feel confident that if so revealed in its fullness, the meagre research I have been able to present will be justified in large part. The conviction behind this belief is that all current (up-to-date evidence) will substantiate in large part if not entirely, the proposed "Thought Experiment" presented herein: That MM Did Not Murder MM.

As to the first part of this work, The Concept of Lying, examined philosophically in light of earlier works (such as Orwell's *Nineteen Eighty-Four*) suffice it to say that I believe I have presented only a working and informal version of the more serious academic work that this theme deserves.

Again, perhaps other more abler hands and minds may pick up the torch of Truth to awaken the weary world as to this onslaught of lies, innuendoes, and untruths that currently have run amuck. But at least I will have done my part (small that it is) to scratch the outer surface.

As to references and Sources Cited in this work, please note the following:

#1: All scriptural citations are from the Authorized KJV (King James Version) of the Bible.

#2: All Quotes cited in this work are taken from the Author's *Great Quotes* series (Volume I and Volume II), unless otherwise stated. These Quote Books may be purchased from the Publisher, Kent Minson at: Y Mountain Press (book@byu.edu).

As these quotes are referenced by Author (in this work), one need only access the "Author Indexing" in these *Great Quotes* series to find the desired citation (and related themes). Or, as many Publishers who refused to publish (my) Quote books have told me: These quotes can typically be found via the Internet, and/or Google Search! (Happy Hunting!)

#3: The 'Eyes of Adolf Hitler' (on the Cover design) is an edited version of an Internet 'pin photo' stated as "Free Download" (i.e., within the public domain) and is therefore without copyright restrictions.

#4: All Quotes from Adolf Hitler (unless otherwise indicated) are from his own book, *Mein Kampf* (written in 1925, but published in 1927: henceforth, referred to as: MK. In 2016, the copyright of *Mein Kampf* expired (according to *Wikipedia*) and is therefore in the public domain. [This work follows the 1943 Ralph Manheim translation, which is in the public domain.]

#5: My copy of George Orwell's book, *Nineteen Eighty-Four,* was published in 1949 by Penguin Books in Great Britain ("Not For Sale in the USA" as printed on the back cover) with a copyright (or "printing") renewal in 1969. I believe it may now be in the public domain.

#6: The "Purist View" referred to in Part One of this work is largely taken from my own Ph.D. Dissertation (pending re-publication later this year) entitled: *"The Concept of Religious Passion: According to Immanuel Kant"*.

#7: Part Four: B. "MM's Last Days on Earth" is largely taken from a book I published earlier last year, entitled: "Which One Will You Feed?" (by Gold Touch Press: available through Amazon.com).

#8: The Chronology of Events in MM's last year alive (1962) referred to (in Part Four) is largely a revised reprint from this selfsame book I wrote earlier (as referenced above).

#9: As to the hundreds of different Sources and References referred to, I am indebted to *Wikipedia* and to U-Tube References (as noted in the "Sources Consulted" section).

#10: The research material I compiled in my original notes are contained in several handwritten notebooks as gleaned from these various (literally, hundreds of) sources. It behooves the serious academic who may wish to carry-on where I have left off to document every footnote, endnote, and jot and tittle.

#11: What I have attempted to do in this work is to portray the Big Picture behind the mysterious death of Marilyn Monroe (as based on these many references).

In the year 2039, these 'details' (or, missing pieces of the 'puzzle') may all come to light. But until then, I maintain that there is an overwhelming probability of updated information to at least dispel the notion that MM Murdered MM.

#12: For the record, I will use **MM**, as shorthand for "Marilyn Monroe"; **MLT**, for the book *Marilyn: The Last Take*; *1984*, for Orwell's *Nineteen Eighty-Four*; Fox, for Fox Studios; **BB**, as shorthand for "Big Brother," **Orwell**, for "George Orwell" (aka: Eric Arthur Blair); **Putin**, for "Vladimir Putin"; **Kant**, for "Immanuel Kant"; **MLL**, for the book *Marilyn: Her Life and Legacy* (Susan Doll; Publishers International Ltd.: 1990); and **MHOW**, for the book *Marilyn: Her Life In Her Own Words* (George Harris, 1995).

#13: References to a certain Box 39 (stored in the Special Collections of UCLA Library and sealed until 01 January 2039) are made by several News outlets including:

(1) On 08 January 2020, by Becky Altringer, entitled: "Marilyn Monroe did not commit suicide, but was murdered." See, www.the_Sun.com ; and

(2) On 09 January 2020, by Ross Ibbetson, entitled: "Mysterious Box of Marilyn Monroe Documents found at UCLA and sealed until 2039 could prove she was murdered." See, www.dailymail.co.uk

#14: Additional background research information on MM's last days and details related to her death can be located in MLT, "Source Notes" (pp.381-414), and in "Sources" (pp.415-433).

Contents

Foreword

Originally, I had wished to include several choice photos of Marilyn Monroe for this work but due to time constraints and delays in Copyright clearance, they were not able to make this Edition.

I had also wished to be able to contact a prominent MM fan, Elton John, who wrote a most charming sonnet to Ms. Monroe, entitled: "A Candle In the Wind" (see, U-Tube Reference, below). Also, Paris Hilton in recent years had dedicated her Tenth Cologne to MM, appropriately entitled: "Tease" (see, U-Tube-Reference, below).

Other luminaries I had hoped to contact included two of my all-time favorite actresses, Gina Lollobrigida, and Jane Fonda. Both actresses knew MM personally! I would have loved to meet (or at least made contact with) either or both of them for this First Edition.

But, alas, time is a cruel taskmaster: This book was slated to come out for the 60th Anniversary of MM's untimely passing, which has a fixed deadline. Perhaps in a Second Edition of this work, I may be able to include at least some of the above good intentions? Time will tell.

Elton John sings tribute to Marilyn Monroe: A Candle in the Wind [2005]
https://www.youtube.com/watch?v=qDT5iQKJt4k&list=RD-MM&start_radio=1&rv=kle2xHhRHg4

Paris Hilton Dresses as MM for "Tease" cologne [13 August 2010]

https://www.youtube.com/watch?v=2gl3ev-r3sA

Paris Hilton honors MM as her 'icon' [13 June 2021]

https://www.youtube.com/watch?v=eyGo78BCI7k

Preface

Although the author of *Nineteen Eighty-Four,* Eric Arthur Blair (25 June 1903-21 January 1950), commonly known by his pen name as George Orwell, was a self-proclaimed atheist, I do not judge his work by that yardstick. True, my work is cast in a Christian culture, as that is how I see my 'Truth'.

But I state for the record that I do not judge the messenger but the message. Again, it's true that the 'medium is the message' to a large extent; however, Orwell has written a genuine literary masterpiece in my view. It is the content, the message, that concerns this work.

To critics who might query as to why this work I've written was not in a more philosophical vein, I can only reply that just as I wrote in English (instead of Russian, for example) because I understand English all the better; so likewise, I communicate my "Truth" in the Christian medium because that is all the world I have come to trust, to know to be true.

This point I make is not an apology for my Christian beliefs (I am not at all ashamed of the Gospel of Jesus Christ). Nor is this point an excuse but merely an explanation. In my view, every author has his or her own biases (or ways of seeing the world) even Orwell.

We each see 'reality' (that 'world point of view') through the subjective spectacles we choose to wear. Once our eyeglasses are removed, we see little as 'real' for even 'reality' becomes uncertain. As a common denominator, we see (and believe to be 'real') only what we can touch, smell, taste, hear or feel with our physical senses. All other senses diminish (or fade) in comparison or appear 'unreal'.

Without grounding in a rock hard (spiritual) foundation (it is my opinion that) we may more easily appear to live in a surreal world of make-believe, to become vulnerable, prime, targets of The Party (whatever the ruling Party may choose to tell us, even twisted truths). If our primal belief-structure (our foundation of everything we hold fast to be true and real) is based on sand (Matthew 7:26-27), then we may find ourselves as 'wandering stars' (Jude 1:12-13; 2 Peter 2:17).

But early instruction in Truth will best keep out error: "Fill the bushel with wheat, and you may defy the Devil to fill it with tares." (Tryon Edwards)

Introduction

This informal investigation into the machinations of the concept of lying presupposes that there is no such thing as a 'private language' (that is, a language that cannot be shared or understood by anyone else).

Furthermore, it is assumed in this work that all languages arise only in public settings, as language is communicated between persons (or, beings) interwoven into our thoughts as *concepts*. No man, no woman, is an island. This social aspect of language is integral to its very definition. Hence, the title of this work as "The *Concept* of Lying".

In coming to a better understanding of the philosophical concept of "Lying", let us examine Immanuel Kant's (1724-1804) concept of 'lying' (commonly referred to as "the Purist viewpoint"). Kant, a German philosopher, was born in Konigsberg, Prussia (now called Kaliningrad, Russia). He was highly respected by all his German, and Polish (Prussian), and Russian students for his exactness in morally upright principles. His viewpoint, as we shall read, was virtually unwavering against the dangers of 'lying'.

In Part One, Section B, we will consider the backdrop to this concept of Lying: "The Cobweb of Lies". I created this term as a spin-off from Willard V. Quine's book, *Web of Belief*, in which he argues that beliefs are like webs in which our individual statements are connected (or depend upon) other statements. Likewise, in the 'Cobweb of Lies', one lie is not enough: You need a backdrop of many lies to maintain the credibility of one Big Lie.

In Part Two, I address the '(Political) Science of Lying'. Firstly, I focus on Orwell's thought-provoking book, *Nineteen Eight-Four,* as an uncanny prophecy of today's New World Order. And, secondly, I apply these Orwellian principles as a playbook to Vladimir Putin's war in Ukraine, and his Russian Rogue Regime.

In Part Three, I use a Thought-Experiment, to analyze a long outstanding Big Lie that is still swallowed today (hook, line, and sinker) by the Mass (and Social) Media: That Marilyn Monroe murdered Marilyn Monroe. To complete this 'thought-experiment' of the Big Lie, to show and demonstrate how this Big Lie is actually that: A big lie, I break down the concept of Lying into its sub-component parts (all 24 of them).

Then in Part Four, having compartmentalized and analyzed the various details of this Big Lie (that MM Murdered MM), I reveal an overview of the last year of MM's life (1962) as a backdrop to her last weekend alive. I then reveal her final days on earth hour by hour to show how it was not feasible that MM would take her own life either by accident or by design.

In conclusion (Part Five), I summarize how it is highly likely that our society could be hoodwinked, lied to, and cuddled into believing Big Lies. The case in point (the Big Lie that MM murdered MM) is used simply as a 'Thought-Experiment' (whether definitively true 100% as presented herein may be a moot point). In the year 2039, we are told that we will know the truth: What really happened to MM?

Just as the Trump era in the USA unveiled the concept of Fake News (reading between the lies), so the Russian propaganda machine has likewise uncovered the Big Lies throughout World Governments.

Now is the time of Reckoning. Now is the time when the Roosters have come home to Roost. Otherwise, now may become the time for Revolution.

For such was the stark warning of a man familiar with the timing of Revolutions, as he states in his own words, in his own book:

> What was--and still is--bound to happen some day, when the stream of unleashed slaves pours forth from these miserable dens to avenge themselves on their thoughtless fellow men! For thoughtless they are! Thoughtlessly they let things slide along, and with their utter lack of intuition fail even to suspect that sooner or later Fate must bring retribution, unless men conciliate Fate while there is still time. --Adolf Hitler (in *Mein Kampf*, p.29)

Part One: The Concept of Lying

A.   The Purist View: Kant

1.   Kant's definition of 'a lie'

The Definition of a lie, according to Immanuel Kant (1724-1804), is "an intentionally untrue declaration to another". He adds that (contra what jurists or lawyers may say) the lie "always harms another, even if not another individual, nevertheless humanity generally, inasmuch as it makes the source of right unusable." ["On a supposed right to lie from philanthropy" (1797); henceforth, referred to simply as "Lies", as translated by Mary Gregor (in *Practical Philosophy*, 1996: p.612). The word 'philanthropy' can also be translated to mean: 'altruistic or benevolent motives'.]

Moreover, Kant adds, one who tells a lie is responsible for its consequences (even before a Civil Court) because "truthfulness is a duty that must be regarded as the basis of all duties to be grounded on contract." To be truthful is a "sacred command of reason prescribing unconditionally, one not to be restricted by any conveniences." (Ibid, p.613).

Mary Gregor adds in the "Introduction" to her translation of Kant's "Lies":

> Kant later distinguished between "what is only formally wrong and what is also materially wrong,"

a distinction that "has many applications in the doctrine of right." In general, people do not wrong one another by doing what would make civil society impossible, but they nevertheless do wrong "in the highest degree" by making the concept of right inapplicable, and with it the concept of a right as distinguished from force. Relying on this distinction, Kant argues that lying is always wrong in the context of right, as distinguished from virtue. (Ibid, p.606)

## 2.	To be Punctiliously Truthful

For Kant, to make a declaration public is equivalent to swearing under oath in a court of law. Indeed, Kant insists that it should not be necessary to swear by oaths, as a man ought to be true as his word. As Kant points out in *Religion Within the Limits of Reason Alone* (1793; as translated by Theodore M. Greene and Hoyt H. Hudson in 1960):

> But it is clearly evident that the wise Teacher who here says that whatever goes beyond Yea, Yea, and Nay, Nay, in the asseveration of truth comes of evil [Matthew 5:33-37], had in view the bad effect which oaths bring in their train: namely, that the greater importance attached to them almost sanctions the common lie. (p.147n.,147)

But Kant is not naive: He recognizes that no one is truly candid. If all men were good, however, people could be candid "but as things are they cannot be" [in Kant's *Lectures on Ethics* (1775-1780); henceforth, simply called "Ethics", as translated by Louis Infield (1930, 1978), pp.224-225].

To state the obvious, people in polite circles at times cannot be punctiliously truthful, as Kant explains:

> But if we were to be at all times punctiliously truthful, we might become victims of the wickedness of others who were ready to abuse our truthfulness. If all men were well-intentioned, it would not only be a duty not to lie, but no one would do so because there would be no point in it. But as men are malicious, it cannot be denied that to be punctiliously truthful is often dangerous. (Ibid, p. 228)

[I am also reminded of Jean Renoir's cinematic masterpiece, *Rules of the Game* (1940), a pensive comedy of errors depicting the members and servants of French society who lie to each other while they secretly play 'the game' of wife-swapping. The aviator Andre (who is, arguably, punctiliously truthful) is mistaken in a lover's tryst for someone else and literally shot to death: He failed to play by 'the rules of the game'].

3.   White Lies

Kant's short treatise on "Lies" was a response to the query asked by a French politician, Benjamin Constant: "Would it be a crime to lie to a murderer who asked us whether a friend of ours whom he is pursuing has taken refuge in our house"? One would think that Kant would agree: "To deceive a deceiver is no deceit" ("Lie", p.611).

No doubt, Kant was aware of the social custom (still prevalent today) in various parts of Europe (including Italy and France) to state an untruth to an inquiring visitor (especially, a stranger) at the door whether so-and-so were home. And as Kant admits that "not every untruth is a lie," the casual reader may understandably be puzzled (or even bemused) as to Kant's candid reply that "a lie is a lie" for not only is a lie "always evil" (in the formal sense), there are "no lies which may not be the source of evil." ["Lies," p. 611; Kant's *Metaphysics of Morals*; henceforth, simply called "Morals", translated by Mary Gregor in 1991: p.227; "Ethics," pp.228-229]

Herbert Herring in *Essentials of Kant's Theoretical and Practical Philosophy* (1993) concludes that Kant's position (in "Lies") is "extremely ignorant (or, purposely ignoring) of the crooked ways and vagaries of our socio-political world". Even Herring's wife calls Kant's position "unrealistic sophistry" (pp.107,115-116).

Before I offer a few thoughts in defense of Kant's rather maligned stance (as a perceived 'prudish purist'), I would like to point out that Kant did believe certain white lies can be justified: "The forcing of a statement from me under conditions which convince me that improper use would be made of it is the only case in which I can be justified in telling a white lie."

And again, Kant says: "If a man tries to extort the truth from us and we cannot tell it him and at the same time do not wish to lie, we are justified in resorting to equivocation in order to reduce him to silence and to put a stop to his questionings." ("Ethics," pp.228-229)

In the example given above, we could respond then to the murderer's question (whether so-and-so is in) with a question of our own: "And if not, what is that to you?". To do so would not be a lie (in the Kantian sense) but as we (deliberately) have not directly answered the question, it would be an equivocation.

To press the issue even further, Kant does permit someone (in exceptional cases) to "make a false statement" (as a deliberate untruth), as he elucidates:

> I may make a false statement when my purpose is to hide from another what is in my mind and when the latter can assume that such is my purpose, his own purpose being to make a wrong use of the truth. Thus, for instance, if my enemy takes me by the throat and asks where I keep my money, I need not tell him the truth, because he will abuse it. And my untruth is not a lie because the thief knows full well that I will not, if I can help it, tell him the truth and that he has no right to demand it of me. (Ibid, p.227)

The issue appears to be an open-and-shut case: Kant permits white lies, equivocation, and even the telling of untruths under exceptional circumstances. Hence (it would appear), he would likewise agree to Monsieur Constant's example that "to tell the truth is a duty, but only to one who has a right to the truth" ("Lies," p.611). But Kant does not so comply.

4.　　The Juridical Context of Lying

This longstanding misunderstanding has arisen, I think, due to a rather technical oversight. What Kant is saying is that "a lie is a lie" (as a tautology, A=A). That is, once we have determined that a given pronouncement is an outright bald-faced lie (in the full Kantian sense of that term), then we cannot wiggle out of our obligation to be truthful and attempt to remedy the situation (as it were) by calling it 'justifiable.' For (next to suicide), a lie to Kant is the greatest violation of man's duty to himself regarded merely as a moral being, "the humanity in his own person" ("Morals," p.225; "Ethics," p.119).

In speaking of 'a lie' in the full Kantian sense of the term, I am referring to Kant's argument [in the First Critique, *Kant's Critique of Pure Reason*, 1781, 1787, 1790; as translated by Norman Kemp Smith in 1933] regarding the "malicious lie" which Kant says is "a voluntary action" (Ibid, A554-555/B582-583).

To be 'forced' to lie, for Kant (on this interpretation) cannot be a lie, as it does not permit a voluntary action. Admittedly, it is this difficulty in determining whether one was 'forced' (or in some sense 'obliged') to tell a lie that becomes the sticky issue, if not a slippery slope in concluding whether one therefore lied.

Liars are held in general contempt, Kant says, because they destroy fellowship. They also are not worthy of happiness, but instead harm themselves immensely in that they not only violate their duty to themselves (as well as to others), they annihilate their own dignity as persons ("Ethics," pp. 118, 224; "Morals,"pp.225,270).

Consistent with the public disgrace due to all liars, Kant believes that the proper remedy for children who tend to tell lies is not to punish them (for they would only become more 'Jesuitical' in their inventiveness). Instead, they should be shamed for their lies. ("Ethics," p.46)

As Constant's example of the murderer at one's door reduced the options of a true-life scenario to but one: 'The necessity to publicly lie,' Kant was obliged to stick to his principles, namely, that of the categorical imperative. [Kant's "categorical imperative" is an universal command or moral law that all humanity must follow regardless of individual or personal desires or circumstances.

This law is worded in Kant's *Groundwork of the Metaphysics of Morals* (1785): "One must act according to that maxim whereby you can, at the same time, will that it should become a Universal Law" (as translated by James W. Ellington, 3rd Edition, 1993, p.30)]

The essential though underlying issue (so presented by Constant), however (according to Kant), was not the necessity of saving one's friend but instead the concept of duty and right with respect to truthfulness. Kant rightly recognized this shift in Constant's position and responded accordingly. What is unfortunate is that casual readers in this brief passage have deemed Kant to be saying categorically that all untruths are lies, and hence no exceptions are to be made.

Kant, on the other hand, distinguishes between 'lying in the juridical context' (i.e., the intrinsic nature of 'duty and right' that Constant refers to), and 'lying in the context of virtue' (i.e., wherein benevolent, altruistic, or philanthropic motives are to be weighed in).

To lie according to the juridical context is to be 'brutally frank'; whereas to lie according to the context of virtue is to be less brutal than frank. A typical example of this 'virtue lying' (the so-called itty-bitty white lie) is to lie when one is asked: "Did you like my cooking, dear?"! To state the 'brutally frank' response shows little regard for one's wife's feelings, as virtue-lying proponents so argue. Hence, the slippery slope conundrum typical of the 'white lie'!

In this latter sense, Kant admits a certain 'prudent reserve' is necessary, although silence can be a 'treacherous ally': "If all men were good, there would be no need for any of us to be reserved; but since they are not, we have to keep the shutters down" ("Ethics," pp.224-225).

In explaining man's 'unsocial sociability,' Kant says:

> Man is a being meant for society (though he is also an unsociable one), and in cultivating the social

state he feels strongly the need to reveal himself to others... But, on the other hand, hemmed in and cautioned by fear of the misuse others may make of his disclosing his thoughts, he finds himself constrained to lock up in himself a good part of his judgments" ("Morals," p.263).

In a down-to-earth sense, Kant could well have responded to the murderer at his door with deception but without (the necessity of) lying, as he explains:

It is possible to deceive without making any statement whatever. I can make-believe, make a demonstration from which others will draw the conclusion I want, though they have no right to expect that my action will express my real mind. In that case, I have not lied to them, because I had not undertaken to express my mind.

In the former sense (that of lying in the juridical context), Kant's position is unwavering, as he consistently sticks to his principles. And for a philosopher, like Kant, consistency is his 'greatest obligation' for "an honest man cannot tell a lie" [Kant's Second Critique: *The Critique of Practical Reason* (1788), as translated by Lewis White Beck, p.23; "Ethics", p.28]

In that sense, telling a lie involves a 'moral imperative,' as Kant explains:

Take, for example: "Thou shalt not lie'! This is no problematic imperative, for in that case it would mean: "If it harm thee to lie, then do not lie." But the imperative commands simply and categorically: "Thou shalt not lie"!

And it does so unconditionally, or under an objective and necessary condition. It is characteristic of the moral imperative that it does not determine an end, and the action is not governed by an end, but flows from the free will and has no regard to ends. The dictates of moral imperatives are absolute and regardless of the end. ("Ethics," p.5)

It does not matter then from the juridical viewpoint what the end or object of lying is all about. Whether one tells a lie for a fortune or for philanthropy, it cannot justify the means ("Ethics," p.44). A 'lie is a lie,' Kant says, and that's that. Hence, Kant's unyielding stance (as that of a Judge in a Courtroom) is seen as 'unfeeling' (even as a Judge must appear impartial in his just judgments).

5.   The Dangers of Inner Lies

In my view, I think Kant was keenly aware of the dangers of inner lies as well as external ones in that the former tends to send out many ripples that are consequently expressed in the latter: Akin to the reaction caused by a pebble tossed into a quiet pond ("Morals," pp.225-226).

Although Kant never read Shakespeare (to my knowledge), I think the sincerity of his moral logic has best been described by Polonius in *Hamlet*: "This above all, to thine own self be true, / And it must follow as the night the day/ Thou canst not then be false to any man" (I.iii.78-80).

For the question could be asked, however, apropos of Kant's insistence that one must not lie, whether Kant himself was lying at the time he wrote that reply. That is, on what basis do we know (or at least 'believe') that Kant was telling the truth when he said 'he would not lie' should a murderer come to his door? This question should not be dismissed lightly, I think, without careful consideration respecting the repercussions of lying.

We believe that Kant was telling the truth simply because we do not know of any instance whereby, he knowingly lied. If Kant had said that it would be morally acceptable to lie (in the Kantian sense), what would be the (furthest) extent of that concession?

We simply cannot know, as a lie is the handle that fits every other vice. It is for this reason, Kant implies that 'the author of all evil' (in the Bible) is not only called a liar but is singled out as "the Father of lies" [John 8:44], lies being the source (or, common denominator) of all evil" ("Morals," p.227).

But one thing we can know: That as Kant remained true to his word, the sincerity of his moral thought has persisted even to this day.

B.   The Cobweb of Lies

1.   What is Truth?

The story is told of the old Greek Philosopher Diogenes who went around Athens in broad daylight with a lit lantern shining it in all the faces of the prominent leaders of Ancient Greece! When asked what did he think he was doing flashing that bright lantern during High Noon into everyone's face, he replied simply: "I'm looking for an honest man!".

Today, we think: Things may not be any different?! Perhaps we still are looking to find that honest individual, that person who can speak the truth without a forked tongue, as the 'redskins' used to say back in the day when the West was wild and free?

Karl Menninger, the President and Founder of the American Psychiatric Association, used to say: "One of the most untruthful things possible, you know, is a collection of facts; because they can be made to appear in so many different ways."

He also added his definition of Truth: "Truth to the lawyer is something one tells or does not tell; to the psychiatrist, it is something that we (or at least 'some' of us) strive wistfully and perpetually to discover; and to others: Something in which they have no interest." (Menninger's *Crime of Punishment*, p.97)

When it comes to an animal that best represents the 'lie,' I think of the crocodile, who when it opens its mouth wide enough to swallow a large prey, releases tears from its eyes, as if it were crying, or feeling sorry, for its victim. Hence, the phrase: 'crocodile tears'!

When I think of a person in history best represented as 'the mother of all liars,' there are so many!

2.　　The Origin of The Big Lie: Hitler

But to choose just a few all-time Big liars, I would say for starters: The Minister of Nazi Propaganda, Josef Goebbels. He said that: "Truth is the mortal enemy of the lie, and thus by extension, Truth is the greatest enemy of the State." What Goebbels was referring to indirectly was his boss, Der Fuehrer, Adolf Hitler's own explanation of the benefits to the 'Big Lie' theory.

As Hitler put it: "In the big lie there is always a certain force of credulity; because the broad masses of a nation... more readily fall victims to the big lie than the small lie, since they themselves often tell small lies in little matters but would be ashamed to resort to large-scale falsehoods" (in *Mein Kampf*, 1927).

The key principle needed to succeed in telling a 'Big Lie' is to not only make the lie Big, but to keep it simple, to repeat it often, until at long last the public will believe it to be true! This process is quite an art, as exemplified in George

Orwell's book, *Nineteen Eighty-Four* (which is discussed at length in Part Two of this book).

In this 'art of lying' one must tell 'deliberate lies,' to genuinely believe in them, so as to be able to forget any fact that has become inconvenient. The chief aim is to preserve 'loving feelings,' and not to be 'brutally frank,' not to tell the 'whole truth,' for to do so would (or could) be perceived to be more 'brutal' than 'frank.'

3.   Slippery Slope of The White Lie

Hence, the creation of the 'white lie,' the lie (as we lie to ourselves) that states only a 'little inaccuracy' so as to save a world of explanation. In so doing, we can see that a 'lie' (as simply an 'alternate point of view') can actually become more (publicly) plausible than the Truth itself!

The art of lying is the art of knowing how to believe lies. As Lord George Byron once said: "And after all, what is a lie? 'Tis but the Truth in masquerade!". To state just a little itty-bitty small lie could be passed off as a 'terminological inexactitude,' or attributed to inaccurate memory, or temporary memory loss, which cannot be held to be a really bad thing after all, as no one can be expected to always have a perfect memory at all times, now can they?

One can easily see the slippery slope involved in justifying these small 'white lies' as no one actually 'lies'. People simply do what they have to do, and say what they have to say, to make their story sound just right. That's all!

Hence, we see that: "A liar begins with making falsehoods appear like truth," (as William Shenstone puts it) "and ends with making truth itself appear like falsehood." But lying is not always done with words alone. It can be done with silence: "For the cruelest lies are often told in silence" (Robert Louis Stevenson).

As John Locke, the British philosopher, so aptly surmised: "Men see a little, presume a great deal, and so jump to conclusions." If the Truth (as it is told) has a very big hole in it, well, we can put into that 'hole' (that 'absence of truth') whatever filler (or lie) we wish, now can't we?! Or, as Bill Vaugh mocks the Truth: "We all want to get 'The News' objectively, impartially, and from our own point of view." We see that when it comes to Fake News, we must learn to read between the lies.

4.   Truth, as the 'Safest Lie'

But for me, Truth is the safest lie, for if a lie is a handle that fits every sin, the misunderstanding behind every truth, then Truth is the only means to set the record straight, let the chips fall where they may!

For what is 'sin' except as the Bible puts it: "He who knows to do good, and does it not, to him it is sin" (James 4:17)! So, there it is: We cannot sin in ignorance, as James says:

Sin is knowing what is true and the refusal to do it, to admit it, to confess it, to let the Truth prevail!

Now, wouldn't it be nice, wouldn't it be easy to spot the liar: If like Pinocchio every time one tells a fib (a real whooper!) that his nose would grow longer and longer? Of course, I'm being just a tad facetious! Everyone knows that 'flatterers look like friends, just like wolves look like dogs!" (George Chapman).

But then, do they? What would happen if people confused what they read in the Newspapers as actual 'News'?! What would happen if people confused Television News with Journalism?! For as we know to be true: Never have so many been manipulated by the Media so much (or so often) by so few!

The dangers with lying 'so often' (to appear perhaps more clever, or to achieve more attention or fame, or power) is that if one does so habitually, he will not only not be able to believe anything told to him, but neither will anyone believe what he says.

It's the "boy who cried: 'Wolf!' too often" syndrome: "When men no longer have the least fear of doing something untrue, they very soon have no fear whatsoever of doing something unjust!" (Theodor Haecker). The danger is that some people (accustomed to lying) may "tell enough white lies to ice a wedding cake" (Margot Asquith)!

On the one hand, there is the argument (as Lin Yutang says): "Society can exist only on the basis that there is some amount of polished lying and that no one says exactly what he thinks"; but on the other hand, "Men are able to trust one another, knowing the exact degree of dishonesty they are entitled to expect" (Stephen Leacock).

If (as Nietzsche argues) "the lie is a condition of life," we need to begin to analyze why it is that so many people today (more so than in the past?) don't want honest answers? Why is honesty not considered by so many (especially political) parties to be the 'best policy'?

Is it because the public does not wish to hear disturbing or unpleasant news? Is it because people believe there is some falsehood mingled with all truth? Is it because (as Hitler argued) that there is 'a certain factor of credibility' in a big black lie as opposed to a little (or small) white lie? Is it because people by and large no longer believe that there is simply one Truth, that a liar can represents two truths (or be a person who lives a double life) simply because s/he 'feels' something to be true irrespective of the facts?

5.   The Scriptural View on 'Lying'

In the Scriptures, it states that a double-minded man is unstable in all his ways (James 1:8; 4:8). The Lord our God does not lie (Numbers 23:19); nor does the Lord make His people to trust in a lie (Jeremiah 28:15).

Indeed, those who 'delight in lies' are cursed of God (Proverbs 19:5; Psalms 62:4) for "no lie is of the truth" (I

John 2:21). Those who plow wickedness and reap iniquity will eat "the fruit of lies" (Hosea 10:13). The Lord God condemns all liars, for no one who "makes and loves to make a lie" can enter into His Kingdom (Revelation 21:1-2,27).

John, the Beloved Apostle, makes it crystal clear that "if a man says, I love God, and hates his brother, he is a liar: For he that loves not his brother whom he has seen, how can he love God whom he has not seen?" (I John 4:20).

Isaiah, God's prophet of Old, states a truth eternal that never can change: "Woe unto them that call evil good, and good evil; that put darkness for light, and light for darkness; that put bitter for sweet, and sweet for bitter! Woe unto them that are wise in their own eyes, and prudent in their own sight!" (Isaiah 5:20-21)

But our Lord Jesus (who is the Christ) perhaps said it best of those (fake) religious leaders of His day (who sought to kill Him): "Ye are of your father the devil, and the lusts of your father ye will do. He was a murderer from the beginning, and abode not in the truth, because there is no truth in him. When he speaks a lie, he speaks of his own: for he is a liar, and the father of it" (John 8:37-44).

Jonathan Swift adds an interesting insight to this prevalence of lies within our society today: "But although the devil be the 'father of lies,' he seems like other great inventors, to have lost much of his reputation by the continual improvements that have been made upon him."

6.   The Essential Elements of 'Lying'

In considering the concept of lying, we do well to note this analysis: "There are three essential elements to a lie: (1) The material must be untrue; (2) It must be known to be untrue; and (3) It must be told with the intention to deceive" (Terence H. Qualter).

Now that is all well and good in a Court of Law, but in the real world, we see that we appear to live in a state not unlike a 'moral earthquake' in which everywhere we may turn, there can be deception abounding. Where can we stand on solid ground, when virtually everywhere we turn to for support is based on the quicksand of lies?!

The only Gatekeeper of what is true, of what is right, of what we can wholeheartedly place our trust and faith in is our Lord, our God! The devil appears to have made a heyday from so many willing subjects who love the spoils of political office, of power, of control over others, of fame, or simply put, who love to lie.

Can we feel comfortable in a world that thrives on the material necessity to lie, to spread propaganda, misinformation, disinformation, and a steady barrage of 'Big Lies'? I hardly think so! As Boris Pasternak, the famous Russian novelist (no doubt speaking of life in the former Soviet Union) puts it so well: "The great majority of us are required to live a life of constant duplicity. Your health is bound to be affected if, day by day, you say the opposite of what brings you nothing but misfortune."

Goebbels once boasted that if he could control the Mass Media (the Newspapers and outlets of communication) of any nation that he would assuredly convert them into "a herd of pigs". Quite the boast!

Yet we see that not everyone can be so easily deceived today, or at least we would like to think so. As the saying goes: "You may deceive some of the people all of the time, and all of the people some of the time, but you cannot deceive all of the people all of the time".

C. The Worst of All Vices--Lying

1. Why is Lying the worst of all vices?

Many decades ago (well into the previous Century), I once heard a Sermon entitled, "The Worst of All Vices" by Joel Nederhood. Alas, I have misplaced the one copy I then had of the full sermon, but a small piece of it was located recently. I herewith submit it to the reader unedited for you to decide: Is lying the worst of all vices?

> The very fabric of our social life is overlaid with a web of falsehood that no one seems very eager to brush away. Our industrial and commercial life benefits from admitted falsehoods that have been used to convince people that they need products which they do not need at all, products which in many cases are more detrimental than useful...

> Today we know that most of us will lie if the stakes are high enough. I heard that one of the rules of the Mafia is that if you want to commit big crimes, don't get caught committing little ones. Bank robbers shouldn't get parking tickets. They shouldn't do anything that would call the cops' attention to them.

> So maybe you are honest when it comes to parking tickets, and paying your grocery bill, and the monthly rent. But would you be willing to lie about something if lying would give you $20,000 or $200,000? Unfortunately, most people apparently would.

It's getting so people think they cannot afford to be honest anymore. Honesty is nice but it's too expensive. In a major city the other day, a key City official was found to be receiving mammoth payoffs from builders. When one of the builders was confronted with the fact, he simply said that the money he had paid him was just part of the cost of doing business in that particular city.

Honesty is nice, you see, but who can afford to be honest? Some contractors think they would have to go out of business if they started being honest. Some retailers believe they would. All kinds of people do. They would like to be honest, but they cannot afford it. And no one else can afford it, either. Thus, Society becomes more and more rotten.

Oh, we have really been fooled on this one: 'Honesty is nice, but it's too expensive!' That's a laugh, really, because think how expensive dishonesty is. Think what we are paying for dishonesty. We are creating a Society in which we cannot trust anybody. Where can one turn nowadays to find an honest man?

You see, we have paid the ultimate price for this dishonest Society we live in. We have surrendered the possibility of having anything that is reliable. Lying has made our world sick unto death! Who can you believe nowadays? Who can you depend on?

Do you enjoy living in a world like this?...

Now, then, when you think about it, isn't it true--lying is the worst vice? It's the foundation of the other vices. It's the most crippling. We pay the greatest price for it.

Lying makes our total environment unreliable. It's like an earthquake, because when you suddenly realize that you are living in a world full of lies, you don't know where to turn anymore. Your world falls in upon your head and you are crushed.

Lying is the worst vice of all.

---Dr. Joel Nederhood, "The Worst of Vices"

2.   The 'Moral Earthquake'

As Dr. Nederhood alluded to, when we live in a world full of lies, it is like a moral earthquake. And when we finally begin to wonder out loud: How did we find ourselves in this moral morass we're stuck in, this quicksand of lost moral values, then we realise how true the old adage is: "The best way for evil to succeed, for evil to grow, as it were, is for good people to do nothing!".

Now we are engaged in major military conflicts across the globe: Like forest fires out of control, these hot spots are not easily quenched. The gnawing even growing sensation is that we as a Civilisation are likely fast approaching the makings of a New World Order...

D. From the Mouth of Babes

1. The Emperor's New Clothes

The Danish author Hans Christian Andersen wrote a folktale (in 1837) entitled: *The Emperor's New Clothes*, now published in over 100 languages! The story is told in many variations today but I like the simple plot as outlined in *Wikipedia* which I hereby present (slightly edited) but which bears re-telling: It involves courtly pride vs. intellectual vanity.

Two swindlers arrive in a major city of a corrupt Emperor who lavishly spends the State funds on clothing and other personal effects. Posing as weavers, these con artists offer to supply the vain Emperor with very expensive clothing that is invisible, they say, to those who are incompetent or simply stupid.

Hired and paid an exorbitant sum of money, these two liars set up looms and go to work. The Court officials and even the Emperor himself visit them occasionally to check their progress. Although everyone can see that the looms are indeed empty, they pretend otherwise, so as not to be thought of as totally inept imbeciles.

Finally, the two scoundrels announce their invisible suit is ready for the Emperor to wear. They mime the dressing of the nude Emperor who then proudly sets off in a royal procession before the entire city to display his glorious attire.

The over-crowded public spectacle soon becomes choked with curiosity seekers, all trying to see how magnificent the Emperors "New Clothes" really are! They all want to see for themselves! But even though they all see the Emperor dressed only in his 'birthday suit', they all proclaim how beautiful his new set of robes are, not wishing to appear stupid.

But stupid they are as a young child blurts out in a loud voice: "The Emperor has NO clothes!". The townsfolk then realize that they have all been duped.

On the face of it, this tall tale appears totally absurd and fit only as a fairy tale for little children. But then one needs to ask: Why has it survived telling and re-telling the world over for so many decades (for 185 years now)? The answer is painfully obvious: To this day, our society has been inundated with lies, outright, bald-faced lies!

But the query persists: Are the peoples of today, in all parts of our global village really making the hard choice to follow their conscience, or do they prefer 'bread and circus'?! That is, to have their Governments take care of them, from the cradle to the grave, to tell them the 'sweet lies' they like to hear: That all is well and that they can trust their leaders to tell them only what is true?

We are reminded of the other child's fable, of a wooden puppet called Pinocchio who preferred to play hooky instead of going to school. He refused to listen to his conscience (Jimminy Cricket) but was persuaded to run away to The Fair with a wily fox and his sidekick, a stray alley cat. And what happened to this blockhead, this silly puppet, you ask?! Well, he literally turned into a jackass, braying like a donkey!

Out of the mouth of babes (Psalms 8:2; Matthew 21:16).

2.   The 'Idols' of Francis Bacon

Francis Bacon (1562-1626), as an English philosopher, tried to explain how it is that so many people tend to believe 'lies'. He devised a means of explaining this tendency through his theory of "Idols". When people turn away from following the truths of the Bible, they turn to 'idols.'

In his Natural Philosophy, Bacon speaks of three such 'idols' which I outline briefly as:

(a) The Idols of the Cave: These idols consist of conceptions or doctrines which the individual cherishes and holds to be dear and near to his heart even though they possess little or no evidence to be true. These 'idols' are so highly prized due to the preconditioning of the individual as based on his education, customs, or experiences (whether accidental or inborn);

(b) The Idols of the Marketplace: These are false conceptions (Idols) derived from public discourse and communication, that overpower our reason and our understanding over time; and

(c) The Idols of the Theatre: These dogmatic idols are like the fictions we view in theatres, where all the world is a stage, but none of the prejudices or biases so inculcated there are ever tested or proven to be true. These beliefs are simply received traditions we accept without question.

In reviewing the writings of Francis Bacon, I'm reminded of the discovery the Apostle Paul made some 2,000 years ago in Athens as he spoke on Mars' hill, that "in all things" the people then were "too superstitious". As the Scriptures narrate: "For all the Athenians and strangers which were there spent their time in nothing else, but either to tell, or to hear some new thing"! (Acts 17:21).

This danger for the General Public (the common folk) to make no serious attempt to cultivate their minds (to master 'critical thinking'), but to prefer superstitions and to spend their spare time in idle gossip ("to hear something new") is, arguably, one of the key reasons that prompted George Orwell to write his futuristic novel, *Nineteen Eighty-Four.*

Part Two: The (Political) Science of Lying

A.   The New World Order: Orwell

1.   Orwell's *Nineteen Eighty-Four*

In 2021, readers of the *New York Times Book Review* rated George Orwell's futuristic novel *Nineteen Eighty-Four* as third in a list of the "Best Books of the past 125 years"! [*Wikipedia*, George Orwell, "Literary Career and Legacy"]

Eric Arthur Blair (born 25 June 1903), more commonly known by his pen name of George Orwell, wrote his earlier work *Animal Farm* in April 1944 (published on 26 August 1946 in the USA). His proposed Preface to *Animal Farm* included the remark: "If Liberty means anything, it means the right to tell people what they do not want to hear."

On that theme (and on 22 May 1946), Orwell retreated to an abandoned farmhouse (known as Barnhill) near the North end of the Isle of Jura (off Scotland's west coast) to begin his pivotal work, *Nineteen Eight-Four* [henceforth, also referred to as simply: *1984*]. Although he completed this book in December 1948, it was not published until 08 June 1949, only months before his premature death at age 46 (21 January 1950).

When but 17 years old, I studied Orwell's final work (*1984*) as required reading in 1971 in order to graduate from High School. Some of the references I refer to in this work are taken from that original copy I still kept all these years. Growing up in a rural community of less than 400 homes, the thought of our Government (as Big Brother) watching us through a Telescreen seemed a bit silly, to be frank.

Even back then, we were still watching black-and-white television. The original series of *Star Trek* which mimicked voice communication through a triangular pin on one's polo shirt seemed 'far out' (the word then used to mean: 'far-fetched').

We did not have cell phones or internet (which were not yet invented). We simply thought that if some yahoo would like to yell at us through our TV screen, we would simply pull the plug. End of Propaganda.

Or so we thought (even 22 years after Orwell's book was published to the world). Today, we are amazed to learn how far-reaching and insightful Orwell's vision of a dystopian future world truly has become. In Orwell's *1984*, his 1948 prediction of 'Newspeak' ('the new political-correctness language to control the masses') to completely replace 'Oldspeak' ('our current language') before the year 2050 now seems more real than ever.

And even though Orwell's prediction of the world as it would be in 1984 did not come to full fruition, it has, arguably, begun to fulfill itself in this Century, as we shall soon see.

2.   Big Brother (BB) is Watching You

[Unless otherwise stated, all page references in this following section are from The Penguin Modern Classics Edition of George Orwell's *Nineteen Eighty-Four: A Novel* (published by Penguin Books in 1954)].

Citizen #6079, Winston Smith (p.188) who is 39 years old (p.98) was married to Katherine from whom he separated over 10 years ago (p.56) because she was "goodthinkful" (a Newspeak word meaning: 'someone who could not think a bad thought', p.108). In Winston's mind, he could not get rid of this marriage to Katherine (arranged by The State; pp. 10, 56-57).

So, he simply abandoned her. He viewed Katherine, not only as his ex-wife (for all practical purposes) but as the most 'empty mind' he had ever encountered: "She had not a thought in her head that was not a slogan, and there was no imbecility, absolutely none that she was not capable of swallowing if the Party handed it out to her" (p.57).

The Party (p.167) referred to was Big Brother ("BB"; pp.17,166), led by the dictator Emmanuel Goldstein, who watched everyone through telescreens (pp.181,188, 226); and whose book *The Theory and Practice of Oligarchical Collectivism* contained the slogans: "Freedom is Slavery" (p.86), "War is Peace," and "Ignorance is Strength" (pp. 144,150).

The Party's Inner Circle and their Thought Police controlled the masses through re-education (in Room 101, for 'slow learners'; p.201), opposing all dissenting opinions. Newspeak is the propaganda machine (to make independent thought impossible) that the Party uses to re-educate the masses into a new way of thinking, to think and to believe whatever the Party tells the public is The Truth (pp.170,200).

As was the case with his ex-wife Katherine, the masses themselves, Winston noted, were not even aware that they were being oppressed and lied to (p.166). As the Party was trying "to kill the sex instinct" in the population (p.56) (for even to confess to have a sexual desire was a "thoughtcrime"; p.58), Winston's extra-marital affair with his co-worker 26-year-old Julia (pp.87, 89, 98, 106-107) eventually involves the Thought Police (who were watching him for seven years "like a beetle under a magnifying glass"; p.222).

Once taken to Room 101 under the Ministry of Love (the place of re-education through torture; p.172,190), Winston considers suicide as a viable option, to use a razor blade. But soon changes his mind as it "was more natural to exist from moment to moment, accepting another ten minutes' life, even with the certainty that there was torture at the end of it" (pp.124,184).

Although he would initially do anything (even to double his own pain in Room 101; p. 191) to save Julia, not to implicate her in his "sexcrime" (to keep his "inner heart inviolate; p.225), he eventually submits to his torturers in

The Ministry of Love "shouting frantically over and over": "Do it to Julia! Do it to Julia! Not me! Julia! I don't care what you do to her. Tear her face off, strip her to the bone. Not Me! Julia! Not me!" (p.230).

Following this confession of crimes typical of Room 101 (real and imaginary; p.193), Winston is told that it is not enough to obey Big Brother: One must love Big Brother. And, even then, it is not enough to be told to love Big Brother, one must voluntarily do so, to love Big Brother of your own free will (pp.204,226,227).

So, the story concludes: Back in the Ministry of Love "with everything forgiven, his soul white as snow," Winston has the feeling of "walking in sunlight" with "an armed guard at his back" as the "long-hoped-for bullet" enters his brain: But it is all right! Everything is all right! The struggle is over! "He had won the victory over himself: He loved Big Brother"! (p.239)

3.   Have Language, Will Conquer

Orwell believed that if a ruling Party controls the language of the people, they will and can control the minds of the people. In order to replace the old language (Oldspeak), it was necessary to create a new language (Newspeak; pp.242-251).

This new language was "designed not to extend but to diminish the range of thought" (p.242). It uses new terms, such as: "facecrime" ('to wear an improper expression on your face'; p.53); "ownlife" ("individualism or eccentricity"; p.69); "unpersons" ("people who not only no longer exist, but who never existed"; p.40); "comrades" (formerly known as "friends"; p.42); "goodsex" (chastity; p.246); "sexcrime" (sexual immorality; p.246); "the Proles" ("the masses or proletariats"; pp.155,166); "Room 101" (the place for re-education for possible re-integration into society under The Ministry of Love, to cure dissidents, to make them "sane"; pp.190-193,203).

In short, "words such as: honor, justice, morality, internationalism, science, and religion simply would cease to exist. A few blanket words covered them, and in covering them abolished them" (p.246). All these 'old' concepts such as liberty, equality, objectivity, and rationality were part of "Oldspeak" and were to be simply replaced (if not entirely eliminated) by Newspeak before the year 2050 (pp.246, 250-251).

4.   Ministry of Truth: The Thought Police

The Thought Police were created in order to destroy the history of the past (pp.19,144), in order to falsify the past. For the (correct, or former) record of history must be stopped. "Nothing exists except an endless Present in which the Party is always right" (p.127).

All facts about past history were to fade away "into a shadow-world in which, finally, even the date of the year" becomes uncertain (p.36). The part and parcel of rewriting History is to eliminate its record entirely. Through this new language "IngSoc" (English Socialism) (p.32), the Past can therefore be controlled.

And as the Party slogan ran: "Who controls the Past, controls the Future: Who controls the Present, controls the Past!" (p.31) As the Past is being continuously rewritten (by the Ministry of Truth), past events "have no objective existence, but survive only in written records and in human memories. The Past is whatever the records and the memories agree upon. And since the Party is in control of all records... the Past is whatever the Party chooses to make it." (p.170)

In Oldspeak, this thinking was referred to as 'reality control'; in Newspeak, it's called: Doublethink (to include "the mutability of the Past"; p.25). The people (the Proles, or the Masses) were to be brainwashed (p.205), their power of reasoning to be destroyed (p.194). They were to be counted as dead, "living without hope", whose "only true life" would be "in the future" (p. 143).

The Thought was all that the Party carried about. And if you did not conform to the Party line, you risked the danger to be brought to Room 101 for re-education, to cure you, to make you "sane" (p.203).

This "system of mental cheating" (p.171) called 'doublethink' involves the concept of 'blackwhite': "The ability to believe that black is white, and more, to *know* that black is white, and to forget that one has ever believed the contrary" (p.170). For in order to rule (and to continue ruling), The Party "must be able to dislocate the sense of reality" (p.171).

To do so, The Party must use "conscious deception while retaining the firmness of purpose that goes with complete honesty. To tell deliberate lies while genuinely believing in them, to forget any fact that becomes inconvenient... to deny the existence of objective reality, and all the while to take account of the reality which one denies" (p.171).

Hence, 'doublethink' is "the power of holding two contradictory beliefs in one's mind simultaneously and accepting both of them" to be true (p.171)!

The "deliberate exercises" of doublethink include:

- **The Ministry of Truth**, which concerns itself with Lies;
- **The Ministry of Plenty**, which concerns itself with Starvation;
- **The Ministry of Love**, which concerns itself with Torture; and
- **The Ministry of Peace**, which concerns itself with War (p.172).

5. Ministry of Plenty: Party Politics

As Orwell envisioned this New World Order, there was no middle-class, only a ruling Party with peasants (or, the working poor). Therefore, a Ministry of Plenty was created that would keep the lower class in check. To achieve this goal, the Party would have to introduce a means of controlling their populace, through a reduction of excesses. For a "hierarchical society was only possible on a basis of poverty and ignorance" (p.154).

The Ministry of Plenty had to therefore work hand-in-hand with the Ministry of Peace. The satisfactory solution (to keep the ruling Party in perpetual power) would be to "keep the masses in poverty by restricting the output of goods" (p.154).

The real challenge, however, is "how to keep the wheels of industry turning without increasing the real wealth" of the people (p.154). The only way to restrict the excessive distribution of these goods was "by continuous warfare" (p.154).

According to The Party: "War is a way of shattering to pieces, or pouring into the stratosphere, or sinking in the depths of the sea, materials which might otherwise be used to make the masses too comfortable, and hence, in the long run, too intelligent" (p.154).

"In principle, the war effort is always so planned as to eat up any surplus that might exist after meeting the bare needs of the population. In practice, the needs of the population are always under-estimated with the results that there is a chronic shortage of half the necessities of life. But this is looked on as an advantage" (p.155).

What is concerned here is not "the morale of the masses" but "the morale of the Party itself" (p.155). The rulers in

The Party become "the priests of power" (p.212). They are solely interested in power for its own sake, not "in the good of others" (pp. 211-212). They prefer instead to make others deliberately suffer through deprivation, "inflicting pain and humiliation" (p.214).

Power to The Party is "in tearing human minds to pieces and putting them together again in new shapes" of their own choosing (p.214), to create a world based on hatred, wherein progress will be "progress towards more pain" (p.214).

No one will dare to trust another, neither his own wife, or children, or friends. There will only be the "intoxication of power" in which there will be no loyalty "except loyalty towards the Party. There will be no love, except the love of Big Brother." (pp.214-215)

The central motive behind this thrust for power that led to the establishment of the Thought Police, the need for continuous warfare, and for the Party itself is left a secret, an unsolved riddle "in the mind" (pp.173, 209).

The only "picture of the future" we are left with is to "imagine a boot stamping on a human face for ever" (p.215)!

6.   Ministry of Love: Room 101

In this world of contradictions, we are told that The Ministry of Love concerns itself with torture, as a form of re-education, or re-integration, into society. It consists of (1) re-learning; (2) understanding; and (3) acceptance (p.209). All dissidents are treated as 'slow learners' who must be re-educated in the torture chambers of Room 101 (pp.101-102).

As described by Winston (our protagonist in *1984*), there were "always five or six men in black uniforms" who would hit at him simultaneously with their fists, or truncheons, or steel rods, or their boots. They would kick him "in his ribs, in his belly, on his elbows, on his shins, in his groin, in his testicles, on the bone at the base of his spine" (p.193).

He would be "flung like a sack of potatoes on to the stone floor of a cell, left to recuperate for a few hours, and then taken out and beaten again" (p.193). But the Will of the State was not simply to wield power over the human body. It was moreover to re-mould the human mind.

To accomplish this feat, of "complete uniformity of opinion on all subjects" (p.165), it was necessary to alter one's view of reality, to have 'reality-control' (now called: "Doublethink"). The target goal of Room 101, and the Ministry of Love, was two-fold: to not only torture the bodies of their victims, but to reshape their minds as well, to "cure" them, to make them "sane" (pp.200-203).

To this end, the Thought Police were instrumental: Once their victim is "cut off from contact with the outer world, and with the past", he becomes "like a man in interstellar space, who has no way of knowing which direction is up and which is down" (p.160). Hence, the "rulers of such a state" can become absolute: They can "twist reality into whatever shape they choose" (p.160).

The only way to defeat this mind control, to achieve true Freedom of thought, according to Winston, was to keep to the secret doctrine that "two plus two make four" (pp.68,176). Winston was aware that logically speaking, the laws of physics could not be ignored. "In philosophy, or religion, or ethics, or politics, two and two might make five, but when one is designing a gun or an aeroplane, they had to make four" (p.159).

But according to the Party's logic: Reality is not external. For whatever the Party holds to be truth, is truth. "It is impossible to see reality except through the eyes of the Party" (p.200). And "in the end, the Party would announce that two and two made five, and you would have to believe it." For "not merely the validity of the experience, but the very existence of external reality, was tacitly denied by their philosophy. The heresy of heresies was common sense" (p.68).

All Winston had to do was to surrender to this 'blindspot' his mind created. In Newspeak, this 'mental blindspot' or "faculty of stopping short, as though by instinct, at the threshold of any dangerous thought" was called "Crimestop". It was a type of "protective stupidity" that included the power "of failing to perceive logical errors" (p.169).

Submitting his mind to "crimestop," Winston could now accept everything, even though the "arithmetical problems raised, for instance, by such a statement as 'two and two make five' were beyond his intellectual grasp" (p.224).

As Winston describes it: "How easy it all was! Only surrender, and everything else followed. It was like swimming against a current that swept you backwards however hard you struggled. And then suddenly deciding to turn around and go with the current instead of opposing it. Nothing had changed except your own attitude... Anything could be true." (p.223)

So, it follows, that if everyone accepts 'the lie' (which the Party imposes), and if all records tell the same tale, then the lie will pass into history and become Truth! (p.31)

7.   Ministry of Peace: Sanity Control

The two aims of the Party (to which The Ministry of Peace was no doubt privy to) were: (1) To conquer the whole structure of the earth; and (2) To extinguish all possibility of independent thought (p.156). As this Ministry of Peace dealt exclusively with 'War,' they worked hand-in-hand with the Ministry of Plenty.

For the object of 'war' in this New World Order was internal: "to keep the structure of society intact" (p.160). The Ministry of Peace interpreted 'war' to be the "sure safeguard of sanity" (p.159). They did not wish to raise the standard of living in the country (p.153), but to create a society in which all men would be considered equal, "to abolish all distinctions"! For "Ignorance is Strength" (p.162).

In this sense, the Party did not see 'war' as an external reality. And, therefore, as 'War' is no longer considered to be "real" (in the Oldspeak sense) but merely an "internal affair" (p.160) (or, at best a struggle "for labor power"; p.152), this 'war hysteria' or 'war enthusiasm' is unfounded.

For "world conquest is believed in most firmly by those who know it to be impossible" (p.172). Nor can we refer to "war" as even "an invasion" because "no invasion of an enemy territory is ever undertaken" (p.158).

At best it seems, this idea of a 'real war' can only be termed a "Special Operation".

B. Russia's New World Order: Putin

1. Putin's New Russia

Are we destined as a Civilization to live in a nuclear winter? Perhaps? We hope not! We pray not! But, like it or not, we as The Western Civilization may truly have a highly unpredictable world-class leader residing in Russia.

Undoubtedly, Putin is a global risk-taker, one who appears to enjoy playing Russian Roulette with world politics. Perhaps, some might say, we well deserve it. Has our indifference, our callous moral feelings to those suffering within our global village led us to this breaking point? This brinkmanship?

For the ice-cold reality is that we are apparently faced with a temperamental tyrant in Rostov-on-Don who (again, like it or not) demands to have his own way. Or else, the world will pay! Dubbed "the unhinged Bully of East Europe", by some; or "a benign Dictator", by others, Vladimir Putin maintains that this current 'war' in Ukraine is not at all 'a war,' nor "an invasion"!

Ukraine is, after all as Putin says, not a sovereign nation, and therefore he cannot 'invade' a country that does not in fact exist. His military presence in Ukraine is but a "special military operation" designed to liberate Ukrainians from their Neo-Nazi Government. Russian troops are simply 'peacekeepers' occupying Ukraine in "an effort to keep the structure of society intact" (see, *1984*, p.160).

Putin's troops are not killing Ukrainian civilians. It is the Ukrainian Nationalists, the Ukrainian Government that is killing their own people! They are known to commit genocide not only in the Donbas (East Ukraine) but throughout Ukraine.

This "special military operation" is 'special' because it is simply a skirmish between Slavic brothers. Ukraine is not a country separate from Russia. Ukrainians are part of Russia. They are 'little Russians' who have gone astray. Putin's "special operation" will free them from their captors and bring them 'home again', back to Mother Russia.

The (current tally of) 15,000 documented cases of Russian war crimes in Ukraine involving the raping, torturing, and killing of Ukrainian civilians is nothing more than Western hysteria, says the Kremlin. Just as American war hysteria believed Russia would 'invade' Ukraine last February, this year, whereas Russia did no such thing!

These alleged Russian atrocities are all staged with actors and Hollywood movie stunts. Nothing they say can be believed. For they claim that Russia is 'at war' with Ukraine but clearly Russia is not at all "at war" with its neighbor, as has already been explained (so states Putin).

Nor did Russia ever "invade" Crimea: She merely liberated Crimeans in 2014 from their Nazi occupiers, the Ukrainians. A country-wide Russian-held Referendum proved that point. Everyone wanted to become Russian citizens in Crimea anyway (or so the story goes).

Likewise, argues Putin, (in the Donbas) in East Ukraine: All Russian-speaking Ukrainians wish to return to their homeland, to Mother Russia, to be free from Ukrainian rule. Russians do not need to worry about their presence in Ukraine today. Because Russia is not the aggressor: The Ukrainians are clearly killing themselves.

To help to cure the Ukrainian people, to make them 'sane,' Russia is providing humanitarian corridors. Already (in April 2022), more than 600,000 Ukrainians in the Donbas have been liberated from their Neo-Nazi tormentors. Because their homes have been bombed by their own Government, led by Neo-Nazis, they are now free to stay in Russian concentration camps.

In these Camps, freely provided by Putin, the fathers are separated from the mothers; the children from their parents; and the brothers from their sisters, in order to present each with his or her own Russian identity, free from the memories of their Ukrainian past, free to become new Russians! For "Freedom is Slavery"!

There is no 'real war' because "War is Peace"! And in Russia there will be work for you because "Work sets you Free" [*Arbeit Macht Frei*]. You Ukrainians who flee to Mother Russia will not starve. We will give you bread to eat and water to drink in our Ministry of Plenty! (The propaganda continues …)

In The Ministry of Love, you will witness for yourselves that we tell the truth. For at all times the Russian Party is in charge of the Truth: Whatever we say is true, and whatever we tell you to believe will become the new Truth. We do not lie.

All that you Ukrainians need to do (as 'little Russians') is to learn, to understand, and to accept the Russian Party line as expounded by our Big Brother, Putin. Those dissidents among you who may not wish to accept this 'new way of life' (our New World Order) need simply to confess all their crimes, even their Thoughtcrimes, both real and imaginary, and they will be cured. It is these thoughts they hold that are hysterical, that are insane.

But we, the Russian Regime, can control your insanity. Reality is not external: It exists within your mind and nowhere else. We can help you to understand that whatever the Russian Party says is true, can be accepted as true (see, *1984*, p.200).

We are here to "safeguard your sanity" (see, *1984*, p.159). You can be cured from the memories of your past history, your past mystical beliefs, your past desires (which are all "Thoughtcrimes"; see, *1984*, pp.19,58) to become sane, to no longer remain a 'slow learner' (see, *1984*, p.201).

Trust us. Believe us. We control the facts of the Past, through which we control those of the Future. And therefore, we control the facts of the Present. We have all the Truth for we control what is true, what is real, what you may or may not choose to believe.

We are Russia. We are the Kremlin. We are the Party. The Party to rule the world: The New World Order.

2.   "Getting Away with Murder": Putin

The question now needs to be asked: Is it Putin or Ras*putin* who is currently leading Russia today? What then is meant by the term, "Ras*putin*", as the alter ego (or 'dark side') of the man commonly known as Vladimir Putin, the President, and Dictator of the Russian Federation. Or, is Putin suffering from a personality disorder akin to: 'Dr. Jekyll and Mr. Hyde'?

As "President Putin", it may appear that Putin is psychologically okay; but as "Dictator Ras*putin*", the query is oft raised: Is he actually a psychopath in disguise? And, if so, what does it mean to be a 'psychopath'?

In our modern era, the most classic case (of a psychopath) was that of Ted Bundy (1946-1989), a rather intelligent young man who appeared in civil society to be (frankly) quite civil, quite normal. But he had a dark side (as is now common knowledge) to kill young women (and even a 12-year-old girl) for no apparent reason. He was, simply put: a full-blown psychopath!

In past years, our Civilisation has eliminated one or two, arguably, psychopathic dictators, namely: Iraqi President Saddam Hussein (in 2006), and Libyan President Colonel Gaddafi (in 2011).

Even a Russian mystic, Grigori Rasputin (1860-1916), was believed by some to be psychotic, if not psychopathic (although he may simply have been 'hypnotic'?). Rasputin appeared to have a 'dark side' to his personality which politically, it is rumored, led to his premature death by assassination. Whether the tag 'Ras*putin*' may be deserved (or, 'reserved'?) for Vladimir Putin time will tell.

Macleans magazine printed a "Special Double Issue" (dated: 04 to 11th of August 2014) with the giant headline banner that read: "Getting Away with Murder". Next to this headline was a large facial photo of Vladimir Putin sporting a pair of dark sunglasses. Underneath the headline, the sub-heading wrote: "Vladimir Putin's Ambitions have now claimed the lives of 298 civilians. Why no one will stop him."

This article tells the story of the downing of Malaysian Airlines Boeing 777 Flight MH17 on the 17th July 2014 (at an altitude of 33,000 feet) as it flew over the pro-Russian occupied territory of the Donbas, in East Ukraine.

All 298 passengers and crew plunged to their death as the Airliner was literally split in two. Although 160 Airline flights had taken place earlier that day over that identical airspace, the targeting of this particular flight was quite telling.

The inside article by Michael Petrou, "Just Try to Stop Him" (p.30), reveals that on 17th July 2014 the Malaysian Airlines Flight MH17 was downed "by Russian-backed separatists using a surface-to-air missile supplied by Moscow" (p.30).

The article goes on to explain this "atrocity" in some detail:

> Rebel leader Igor Strelkov, believed by Kyiv to be a Russian agent, posted a tweet bragging about

shooting down the plane, which he thought was an Antonov An-26 transport aircraft of the type that had already been shot down over eastern Ukraine earlier this month [in July 2014]. 'We warned you--do not fly in our sky," he said, before removing the tweet when it emerged the rebels had, in fact, killed almost 300 civilians (p.30).

The sub-headings and large boxed captions throughout Petrou's article explains how Putin can (and did) "Get away with Murder," as follows:

(1) "Just Try to Stop Him": Why even the horrific downing of an airliner and the international condemnation that followed won't slow Putin's ambitions. (p.30);

(2) "Blood on his hands": Ukraine, for Putin is not an issue on which he will easily cede ground (p.31);

(3) Russian money still fuels London's financial district. Germany still runs on Russian gas (p.32);

(4) If the Europeans aren't prepared to crank up pressure, a lot more weapons flow into Ukraine (p.33);

(5) Putin's popularity seems to be sky-high. A lot of this is because Russian public opinion is shaped by Russian media. Most Russian media, especially television, are controlled by the State... The domestic media picture that you get in Russia is just so utterly alien to what we *know* to be the facts on the ground' (p.34).

To all intents and purposes, it clearly appears that (for some time now): Orwell's predicted New World Order has not only found root but is beginning to flourish in Putin's New Russia.

As noted by one of Russia's senior Diplomats who officially resigned in protest on the 24th May 2022, for the following reasons:

> For twenty years of my diplomatic career, I have seen different turns of our foreign policy, but never have I been so ashamed of my country [Russia]... Those [in the Putin Regime] who conceived this war [against Ukraine] want only one thing: To remain in power forever, live in pompous tasteless palaces, sail on yachts comparable in tonnage and cost to the entire Russian Navy, enjoying unlimited power and complete impunity. To achieve THAT they are willing to sacrifice as many lives as it takes." --Boris Bondarev

Part Three: The Big Lie—'MM Murdered MM'

A.   The Big Lie: As a 'Thought Experiment'

1.   The 60th Anniversary of MM's Death

Sixty years ago, on the 4th of August 1962, Marilyn Monroe (MM) was found dead in her home in Los Angeles, California. She was 36 years old. The purported widespread belief was that she committed suicide. No one wanted to believe it was true. Everyone who was close to her denied that it was even possible. The events and details surrounding her death were thought to be suspicious at best. Rumors spread that there was a major cover-up. [MLT, pp.315,326,244-345,373]

A lot of people were implicated: The Kennedy brothers (JFK and RFK) who had intimate ties with MM; J. Edgar Hoover, head of the FBI who clearly detested her (MLT, p.372); LBJ, Lester Baines Johnson, who had close ties with J. Edgar Hoover; the CIA (*Marilyn*, by Norman Mailer, p.374; MLT, p.414); Mafia connections tied to Frank Sinatra; even that Sam Giancana, the Chicago Mafia boss, had it in for the Kennedys and simply arranged MM's murder to implicate both those men he so openly loathed (MLT, p.285). And the list goes on.

This book, based on my personal research into the information we, the public, have on MM's life in 1962 leading up to her untimely death, purports to show that MM was murdered. No, it was not self-murder. It was cold-blooded deliberate murder, with real intent.

These findings, I will admit, may not be accepted by all readers. But my point is not that I have all the answers, or that I can prove beyond a shadow of a doubt that the people and motives behind MM's murder (as I will disclose in Part Four) are 100% correct; or, what I will disclose is the only possible option: But that until now (based on the research I have achieved) I do not know of a better alternative, or answer.

Yes, some sources claim that the FBI and CIA records regarding MM's murder will all be de-classified and released to the public in 2039. How this date was ever arrived at, frankly, is beyond me?! Why the long delay? What is there to hide?

We saw what happened when the secret files on the murder of John F. Kennedy (JFK) were (promised to us) to be released when Donald J. Trump was US President. It never happened. The DOJ (Department of Justice) simply refused to cooperate with the Trump Administration's request for full disclosure, citing "National Security" (or some such rot!). So, don't hold your breath until 2039!

But let us create a 'thought experiment', something that philosophers are accustomed to inventing when they seek to solve difficult mysteries. Let us assume (for the purposes of this 'experiment') that MM was murdered in cold blood. Let us see where this 'thought experiment' will take us. Are you ready for the trip? Okay, all systems go! Let us begin.

2.   Dial MM for Murder

As with every murder investigation, it is important to know of the events or particulars that occurred prior to the murder scene. That is, in this 'thought experiment', it may be useful to dissect (or analyze) the subcomponent parts involved in this 'concept of lying' in MM's life prior to her murder. There are least 24 sub-categories to this concept (lying) that I have been able to compile.

We will look at these composite parts in Section C of Part Three, to come to understand the 'cobweb of lies' surrounding MM's life. She was lied to on so many levels. As we shall see, her own murder (and subsequent, autopsy) were covered in lies, including the Big Lie, that she died of her own hand, or choosing.

This Big Lie, I maintain, is perhaps one of the biggest 'mother of all lies' in the 20th Century. But again, I maintain, there are so many more Big Lies all around us. Indeed, not to sound paranoid but I think we are not out of the woods, so to speak, even if we can conclude that MM was indeed murdered in cold blood.

As an example, to reveal how those who knew MM personally (and up close) felt about her passing, I found the Testimony of George Barris (1922-2016), the last photographer to have had a photo shoot with MM (13 July 1962) only weeks before she died, quite revealing.

I quote his Testimony from his book, *Marilyn: Her Life In Her Own Words* (Citadel Press: 1995), as follows:

> Why have I waited all these years before deciding to have this book published? I was in a state of shock after Marilyn died... I will never believe that she took her own life. It will always be my conviction that she was murdered. (p.xvi)

B.   'Thought Experiment': Background

1.   'Big Lie' Discovered

While working on my earlier book, *Which One Will You Feed?* (involving the murder attempt on my life in 2018), I came across the theme of 'lying'. (This 'concept of lying' was one of thirty-four basic concepts I was researching then). In particular, I realized in my research that the death of MM was not accidental, nor did she kill herself deliberately. This 'fake news' assumption turned out to be a truly 'Big Lie'! She was in fact: murdered!

As the details of that unfortunate and untimely death (murder) became apparent, I marvelled that no other writer had put together all these pieces of MM's puzzling death, until now, as revealed in my unintended research into her heretofore 'mysterious murder'. Or, at least, I was not aware of any such work at the time.

2.   Second Witness: *Marilyn: The Last Take*

As I contemplated on MM's 'suspicious death', I seemed drawn to investigate everything related to MM's death (almost like the proverbial 'moth to the flame'). Then out of sheer luck, I spied a book entitled, *Marilyn: The Last Take* (1992), in a used bookstore.

I could not believe my good fortune! I quickly bought it and read its contents somewhat avidly, I'll admit! "Could it be," I thought, "that finally some other research team came to the similar conclusion that I did?".

My research was based until then on what was available in the public domain: researching literally hundreds of Google searches both in U-Tube and through *Wikipedia*. I had put together a timeline (a chronological history) of MM's last few months in 1962, focusing specifically on her last two weekends alive.

I was quite stunned, frankly, how in so many ways both this new-found book, *Marilyn: The Last Take* (written by Peter Harry Brown and Patte B. Barham and published by The Penguin Group: 1992; hereafter, referred to simply as: MLT), and my own prior research fell into line.

If I had not written previously what I did in my own personal research on this subject, I could well understand how an outsider could conclude that my research was based solely on this one volume alone. But I do maintain that it was not.

To be expected, there were discrepancies, there was not total agreement on all points discussed. I had to fill in a lot of missing blanks or gaps that this (otherwise, excellent) book had not yet discovered regarding MM's timetable in 1962, especially the fine details regarding MM's murderers (the way she was murdered, the likely motives for this deliberate killing, and so on). Because MLT was published before the disclosure of these details (especially, by the

Giancana Family) regarding MM's murder, the case of who murdered MM was left open in MLT.

3.   Not a Conspiracy Theory

Putting all these pieces together (as based on my earlier extensive research), I then realized (in 2021) that quite likely I had enough raw material to form the basis of another book, to bring to light the Big Lie that 'MM had murdered MM'.

But due to unexpected delays (the Covid-19 pandemic, the Delta variant last year, and now in February, the invasion of Ukraine, all of which resulted in the continual postponement of connecting with my wife-to-be in East Ukraine), the writing and composition of this book was delayed until now. And perhaps for a good reason, as this book has taken quite a different (and deeper) thrust in its theme due to recent political events.

Today, I am content to have finally published my findings on Miss Monroe's unseemly death on the 60th Anniversary of her passing. I am aware of so many conspiracy theories regarding that awful event. But, I maintain, that this book is not another 'conspiracy theory'. It is a heartfelt and academic attempt to put together the timeline of events leading to MM's death, and to include some of the details immediately thereafter, as the reader may note.

Although I have consulted and researched hundreds of sources and materials (from virtually every possible place found in the public domain), I have not had the time to carefully document (chapter and verse) where every phrase, sentence, and tidbit of information came from: More work needs to be done in order to make this 'murder investigation' more thorough, more convincing, more professional, I do readily agree.

However, I do supply the references (the 'raw materials', so-called) I used in my research (the end results of which I had handwritten in my several keytabs of personal notes) for other writers to pick up the challenge, to complete the task I have only just begun.

[The long list of references I used in *Wikipedia*, the list of U-tube References, and other sources are placed at the end of Part Four.]

My dream is the hope and prayer that another (younger or more experienced) researcher, or team of researchers, will do greater justice to the memory of MM than I have.

May God bless that endeavor, for the Truth must prevail despite this incessant cesspool (or cobweb) of lies that have surrounded MM for far too long!

4.   Parallel Research: Similar Results

In filling in (some of) the details of MM's last weeks on earth, I have been pleased to see that my personal research was headed in the 'right' direction. When I reflect upon the near-parallel research done by the MLT authors, I am reminded of the events that occurred in the discovery of the light bulb. Apparently, two (or more) scientists working on the similar invention (or, discovery, as in medical research) may come to the similar (or, sometimes identical) conclusions.

The credit as to which scientist actually (first) discovered the light bulb may be a useful analogy here. Many people (including myself, until recently) held the common belief that Thomas Edison (1847-1931) was the first to discover the electric light bulb?

But, according to *Wikipedia:* "In 1840, [Warren de la Rue] enclosed a platinum coil in a vacuum tube and passed an electric current through it, thus creating one of the world's first electric light bulbs" ("Warren de la Rue: Biography"). Edison was only 7 years old then when Warren de la Rue (1815-1889) first discovered the electric light bulb, it seems.

But another writer, Paul McLellan seems to dispute both inventors: He claims that perhaps Nikola Telsa (1856-1943) might be credited with that discovery.

[See his article, "Telsa vs. Edison: Who Really Invented the Light Bulb?"; 08 May 2018 in: www.lightbulbs.com.]

In this particular work, I will maintain two things:

(a) that I am interested in getting to the bottom of MM's highly suspicious death regardless of the origin of this or that source: For Truth is Truth no matter the source, just as gold is still gold, even if it is found in the mud; and

(b) that my personal research and conclusions were made prior to my reading of this surprisingly similar work, MLT.

5.   The Testimony of Two Witnesses

The main reason for stating what I hold to be true: That I compiled all the research (through other sources) on the events leading to MM's death prior to discovering (and reading) the MLT book is that it confirmed (in my own mind, at least) that there was a Second Witness collaborating the direction of my own painstaking research. Hence, the 'probability' (and not mere 'possibility') that my research was actually on track and accurate was significantly reinforced.

What I hope the reader to take away from these accumulated findings in my own research (to ultimately determine the cause and nature of the circumstances in MM's death) is to revive an interest, or at least a spark of serious curiosity, in the minds of other (potential) researchers, to carry on the torch of enlightenment and truth concerning this grave injustice done to MM's memory and reputation.

She did not commit suicide: She was in fact murdered. The results of my research end with that conclusion. Let the events of her life and the combined results of these Two

Witnesses (the research of the MLT book, and my own) speak for themselves.

For now, and until the currently secret records and extensive classified files on Ms. Monroe's death are exhaustively exposed (and de-classified) to public view, I will leave my findings (such as they are) to the conclusion the reader himself (or herself) may draw.

I rest my case.

Lying:

Beguiling	Hypocritical
Crafty	Inaccurate
Cunning	Insincere
Deceiving	Loquacious
Defrauding	Mendacious
Dishonest	Plagiarizing
Equivocating	Propagandizing
Exaggerating	Saying-white-lies
Excusing	Serving-'father-of-lies'
Falsifying	Stating-whoppers
Forked-tongue	Taking-unfair-advantage
Full-of-trickery	Untruthful

C.   The 'Cobweb of Lies' Told to MM

1.   The 'Concept of Lying' Analyzed

In this Thought Experiment (to demonstrate that MM did not murder MM), we can unravel this cobweb of lies surrounding MM, lies that not only (arguably) tried to fashion her into something or someone she was not, but that led to her untimely end.

In the following 24 subcategories, we will see that to each aspect of 'This Concept of Lying', MM has been lied to. This background evidence points to the consistency of creating a cobweb of lies not only for MM when she was alive, but in the cover-up relating to her death. Let us proceed with this analysis, to unpack the structure of lies weighing down on MM. [All citations from the book *Marilyn: The Last Take* are hereafter referred to simply as: MLT.]

2.   The Beguiling Lie

To be 'beguiling' is to be 'charming or enchanting, often in a deceptive way.' In this regard, we can see that the movie director, George Cukor (1899-1983) who had directed MM in *Let's Make Love* (1960) was obliged by Fox to direct MM again in their last movie together *Something's Got to Give* (1962). Cukor, an openly Gay Director, had pretended he liked MM during the set of this last movie they did together.

But as MLT affirms: Cukor loathed and even downright hated MM with an unrelenting passion (because as rumors still have it, he was snubbed by bi-sexual Yves Montand in *Let's Make Love*, who clung onto MM instead) [MLT, pp.28-33,60,114-116].

Pretending to be charming and enchanting towards MM, Cukor had MM re-do dozens of retakes of the same scene even though the scenes (to later viewers) appear perfectly flawless. [MLT, p.36]

But Cukor's aim was apparently to demoralize MM and to have her fired, which dismissal he apparently succeeded in doing as noted in his letter to Fox dated 06th June 1962 in which he stated, "She [MM] is a spoiled pampered Superstar and represents all that is bad about Hollywood today." MM was fired two days later on 08th June 1962. [see also, MLT, pp.52,175-177,199]

3.   The Crafty Lie

To be 'crafty' is to be 'clever at achieving one's aims by indirect or deceitful methods'. Fox in their intent to fire MM (arguably, "one of the most financially successful stars in Fox's history," MLT, p.190) had to find a crafty way to justify their position. So, they set out to destroy MM's reputation as a superstar.

"The publicists dredged up two of Marilyn's most private heartbreaks: her fear of insanity, and her long-hidden history of learning disabilities. Cleverly and insidiously, they turned these faults into a firestorm." (MLT, p.219). Even George Cukor, MM's director, wrote to Fox that MM "the poor dear has finally gone around the bend" (MLT, p.217). Monroe was depicted as "half-mad" (MLT, p.211).

Then the knock-out punch came from Fox's own Chief of Production, Peter G. Levathes, to *The Times* that: "Miss Monroe is not just being temperamental: She is mentally ill, perhaps seriously" (MLT, p.215).

4.   The Cunning Lie

To be 'cunning' is to be 'sly, or evasive, to be resourceful, and scheming, especially in tricking someone into believing that something appealing (or cute) is for their own good, even though it may not be.'

When MM was acutely sick with a massive sinus infection in May 1962 (diagnosed as 'dangerously ill' with 'chronic sinusitis') and suffering a fever of 101 degrees, dizziness, unbearable headaches, and lethargy, Fox arranged drugs for her (called: 'hot shots') to be given to her twice daily to artificially shock her back to health. These injections "contained methamphetamines, a few vitamins glucose to give an immediate lift, and a small amount of Librium to smooth out the effect of the uppers" (MLT, pp. 81-82).

But man-made chemical pills were merely another tool to keep MM working far beyond her normal body tolerance (MLT, pp.83-84).

As this was MM's last film with Fox, their Executives' attitude (especially that of Phil Feldman's) as related by MM's physician, Lee Siegel, was (to quote them verbatim): "Let Marilyn collapse after we finish"! (MLT, p.81). This treatment was not uncommon in Hollywood having been used with marked success particularly with racehorses when the stakes were high and the horse's life after the race is of no consequence to its owners.

5.   The Deceiving Lie

To be 'deceiving' is 'to cause someone to believe something that is not true, typically in order to gain some personal advantage'.

On the 16th of December 1961, MM was told by Fox that she had to complete one more film entitled: *Something's Got to Give* in order to be released from her movie contract. She tried to refuse to make any more movies with Fox (especially after her disastrous relationship with Director George Cukor in *Let's Make Love*, shot in 1960).

But her lawyer Milton Rudin advised MM that she had no choice, legally speaking. Even her Swiss-trained psychoanalyst, Ralph Greenson, persuaded MM that she 'should work' for her 'emotional health' (MLT, p.44).

Later in hindsight, we can see that this advice which they gave was deceptive: Both men were actually persuaded by Fox to coax MM to work for them. As it turned out, the one movie director MM did not enjoy working with, George Cukor, was also ordered by Fox to direct MM in this 'last film' together.

To agree to work for Fox (especially under this set of circumstances) was anything but good for MM's "emotional health" despite what her highly paid psychoanalyst claimed. Nor did MM have to work on this particular movie for Fox as her 'last film.' (MLT, pp.214-215)

When MM discovered this 'betrayal' by her own support group, she determined to fire all of them, as Fox ended up terminating their contract with her anyway. (MLT, pp.223-224)

6.   The Defrauding Lie

To 'defraud' is to 'trick or to cheat someone in order to obtain money from them, or to cheat someone out of something of value'. A defrauder can be 'a double-dealer, an imposter, a fast-talker, or slick smooth wheeler-dealer, a quack or shamster.'

In this sense, we can see that MM finally came to realize that her so-called 'support group' (which she treated as her 'substitute family and) to whom she paid a lot of money for their services, was actually not working for her own behalf, but for their own self-interests. She saw that they had "done more harm than good' despite the fact she generously paid them to protect her interests, as professionals.

MM felt that she should dismiss all the following 'family members' from her payroll (as they did not properly protect her from being fired from Fox): Pat Newcomb (her so-called publicist, who was secretly a liaison for Bobby Kennedy); Paula Strasberg (her drama coach, whom MM was paying $3,000/week for her services); Ralph Greenson her psychoanalyst (who charged MM $1400/month for his services); Eunice Murray (her so-called housemaid hired by Dr. Greenson, was secretly a psychiatric nurse who collected negative data on MM), and the list goes on. [MLT, pp.205-207,220,241-242,278]

7.   The Dishonest Lie

To be 'dishonest' is 'to be untruthful, crooked in one's dealings, not fair with the facts, to be corrupt, not relaying accurate information, (typically as it relates to one's character or behavior especially in a relationship), to perpetuate a deliberate mistake or misunderstanding, to deliberately withhold information, or simply not to tell all the truth or information in order to skew the perception of something or someone in a misleading way, to be treacherous.'

When Fox shut down the production of *Something's Got to Give* on the 06ᵗʰ June 1962 (without informing MM), she still was led to believe that they would resume production on the 11th of June. But instead, she had to be told by her psychoanalyst, Ralph Greenson, on the 08th of June 1962 that she was indeed fired effective that very day! (MLT, p.223)

Fox told MM that they were firing her because she was causing a huge financial loss to their Studios. They cited that she did not work on all the days she was supposed to, even though she had documented doctor's notes to indicate she was sick for most of those days.

And although between the 21st of May and the 1st of June, MM worked 9 days and completed 10 key scenes, Fox did not acknowledge her commitment to the film. [MLT, p.169] On the day of MM's 36th birthday, 1st June 1962, Fox had her work until 6 p.m. as if she were "a bad child" (MLT, pp.176-177). They wanted their 'pound of flesh' from MM even though they were paying her a rock-bottom salary of only $100,000 to make the film.

By contrast, Elizabeth Taylor was paid $1,000,000 to make *Cleopatra.* And Richard Burton, her co-star in that film, was paid full salary even though he "worked only five times in the first seventeen weeks, and only thirty days in the entire first year" (MLT, p.97). Fox, if the truth be told, was losing a lot more money on *Cleopatra*, than on *Something's Got to Give!* (MLT, pp.91-95, 97)

Fox lied to MM. They were dishonest. They had intended to fire Elizabeth Taylor on the 8th June 1962 (on the same day MM was fired), because her expenses were going through the roof.

Her living costs alone reached $228,000 (more than double MM's entire salary for *Something's Got to Give*). Liz Taylor's overtime rate (at $10,000 per day) along with 10% of the gross income (whether or not the film turned a profit), and her insistence that *Cleopatra* be filmed in Todd-A-O, "the wide-screen process created by her late husband, Michael Todd" ensured that her initial $1,000,000 salary more than double to a final profit (to include royalties, etc.) estimated to be: $7,000,000! (MLT, pp.91-95,182,202).

But Liz Taylor threatened to sue Fox and to tie up *Cleopatra* for years if she were fired! (MLT, p.187). Her ruse worked. Because the Fox Executives couldn't get rid of Taylor, so they decided to show "they were strong men and fired Monroe, in Taylor's place"! (MLT, p.187)

8.   The Equivocating Lie

To be "equivocating" is 'to use ambiguous language so as to conceal the truth of to avoid committing oneself'.

On the 17th of April 1962, MM received an official invitation from the White House (from RFK, Bobby Kennedy) to attend JFK's 45th Birthday Gala held jointly at the Democratic National Convention on Saturday the 19th of May. When

MM requested permission from Fox to attend the Gala (at Madison Square Garden in NYC), they initially replied in the affirmative (though not 'officially').

Later, they would 'equivocate' on their permission to grant MM a 'leave of absence'; but instead demanded that MM work even on Saturdays (to include the 19th of May). Because MM received reassurances from RFK that he would soothe the feathers of Fox (to ensure that she would not be fired), MM left for the Gala event.

A few weeks later, she was fired from Fox for going to JFK's Birthday Gala without 'official' permission! [MLT, pp.129,132-135]

9.   The Exaggerating Lie

To lie with 'exaggeration' means 'to represent as larger, better, or worse than things are in reality'.

On the 8th of June 1962, Fox officially fired MM ("one of the most financially successful stars in Fox's history"; MLT, p.190). They charged her with a $500,000 lawsuit (five times the salary they initially promised to pay her to do this last film for them) on the grounds that she violated her Fox Contract: Not showing up for work when they 'required' her to do so. (MLT, p.246)

Fox was upset that MM's (total time of) three weeks off work cost them almost $100,000 in production costs (as they had 104 employees on the set). Their argument was most clearly a gross exaggeration.

What Fox did not disclose, however, was that MM's chief Fox rival, Elizabeth Taylor, had cost Fox Executives $8,000,000 (that's eight million dollars!) due to her "bout of pneumonia and bronchitis" which delayed the production of *Cleopatra* for seven months! (MLT, p.78)

10.   The Excusing Lie

To lie with excuses is 'to attempt to lessen the blame attaching to a fault or offense, to seek to defend or justify one's position'.

The excuses the US Security Services (subsequently) made to bug and wiretap MM's Brentwood home in L.A. (without telling her, of course) was that they had to do so for National Security reasons. As MM had purchased a rather dated house, it needed to be rewired. The people hired to so do (secretly contracted by the FBI and CIA) lied to MM that they were there to simply 're-wire' her home. (They had deliberately given her a price estimate she could hardly refuse).

The logic or reasoning the Secret Service (later) used was to argue that they had to know where their President was at all times, as they had 'the nuclear suitcase' with them (due to political tensions with Cuba at that time). As JFK would repeatedly 'duck' from these Agents (to rendezvous with his various 'sweethearts'), wire-tapping the homes of his 'lovers' was thereby justified. [MLT, p.217]

11.   The Falsifying Lie

To falsify means: 'to alter information or evidence so as to mislead, to allege a purpose for doing something when in fact an ulterior motive is the actual underlying reason.'

Bernard Spindall (formerly from the Military Signal Corps) and Fred Kotash (a private detective), among others, falsified their motives for offering to re-wire MM's older-style Brentwood home in L.A.

As it turns out, these 'wire specialists' were actually con artists who wiretapped and bugged MM's home to include orders from: (1) J. Edgar Hoover, head of the FBI; (2) the CIA; (3) Jimmy Hoffa (of the Teamsters' Union); and (4) Sam Giancana, a Chicago Mafia boss. (MLT, pp.254,308-309)

12.   The Forked-Tongue Lie

To lie "with a forked-tongue" is an old expression from the Cowboy-and-Indian days of the Old West to mean that 'one is double-dealing, working to people's disadvantage behind their backs, to be a back-stabber, to be duplicitous'. It originates from the biblical analogy that, like the snake, the Devil has and speaks with a 'forked tongue.'

When Fox shut down the *Something's Got To Give* set on the 6th of June 1962, they left the impression with MM that they would begin re-shooting the script on the 11th of June. But they spoke with 'a forked tongue'. Their intention was to immediately fire MM which they did on the 8th of June. They never even bothered to tell MM she was officially terminated. They left that task to her psychanalyst, Ralph Greenson, to do.

MM was "cushioned by a false sense of security" by her own support group (her 'substitute family') whom she would later dismiss from her payroll for they clearly did not protect her from being fired from Fox. They were perceived (perhaps correctly so) as being 'back-stabbers'. (MLT, pp.205-207,241-242)

13.   The Full-of-Trickery Lie

Full of trickery is an expression that alludes to the 'practice of sneaky underhanded ingenuity with the purpose to dupe or to cheat'.

When Bobby Kennedy had to attend several conferences in L.A. for the weekend of July 27 to 29th, he did not wish MM to be there to possibly upstage his public appearance for his pending movie production, *The Enemy Within* (based on a book he had written in 1960). He therefore prevailed on Pat Lawford (Peter Lawford's wife, and his sister) to coax MM out of town during this visit.

The Lawfords did so, taking MM to accompany them on a weekend jaunt to Lake Tahoe (ostensibly to attend Jack Jones' opening at Frank Sinatra's lavish Cal-Neva Lodge). Monroe later told Robert Slatzer that the Lawfords had tricked her into leaving L.A. (MLT, pp.282-284)

14.   The Hypocritical Lie

Hypocrisy, simply put, is the 'practice, actually pretense, of claiming to have moral standards or beliefs to which one's own behavior does not conform, whose actions belie his own code of ethics or values'.

Generally, we hear of hypocrisy as the action of not practising what one preaches, not being true to one's moral code or public image. We often hear hypocrites say: "Do as I say, not as I do!". For MM this hypocrisy was so painfully and shamefully evident in the treatment of her bona fide illness(es).

Fox Executives could take time off for as long as they needed it when they were under the weather, but not MM. She was expected to work regardless of her emotional state, mental health, or physical condition. To push her along, they would give her 'hot shots' and other drugs required to force her to work far beyond her "normal body tolerance" (MLT, pp.74-84).

15.   The Inaccurate Lie

To be 'inaccurate' in lying refers to 'the tendency to be imprecise, mistaken, unreliable, untrue (also, unfaithful as to the facts), wrong, counterfactual, fallacious, inexact, off base, specious, defective'.

The concern with misrepresenting the facts is that it can be done though innocent error (an 'honest lie'), or through the intent to deceive or to falsify figures, and facts. To be "inaccurate" in presenting one's testimony in a Law Court, for example, may lead to charges of perjury.

On the last day of MM's life, she receives a veritable flurry of phone calls. (Many of those calls have not yet been declassified from her phone log, as they are still retained in the FBI secret files.)

But we do know that at 6 P.M. Ralph Roberts (her masseur) called her for the third time. His call is intercepted by Dr. Greenson who bluntly barks out to Roberts that MM is 'not home'.

This statement was a deliberate lie. It was not accurate: MM was home, but the call was not given or forwarded to her for unknown reasons. The unpleasant tone of voice to Roberts bothered him, as well as the inaccurate lie that MM is 'not home.' He muses that at least Greenson could have been more polite and said simply: "MM is not available" or that "MM is busy at this time."

16.   The Insincere Lie

Insincerity is the 'tendency to not express genuine feelings.'

They say that 'all is fair in love and war', and I suppose that proverb is certainly true in the case of RFK and MM. 'If one plays with fire, one may risk being burned' is a truism oft repeated in these affairs of the heart, especially the extra-marital ones, no doubt. And so, it is no big surprise to learn that MM was lied to with the most slick insincerity one could imagine.

The movie star Laurence "Larry" Olivier (who was no stranger to these sorts of extra-marital matters) commented about his extra-marital affair with Vivien Leigh:

> I couldn't help myself with Vivien. No man could. I hated myself for cheating on Jill [Olivier's current wife] but then I had cheated before, but this was something different. This wasn't just out of lust! This was love that I really didn't ask for but was drawn into. (*Wikipedia*, "Laurence Olivier")

"Larry" Olivier then commented on what he believed was the secret of an actor's success. He replied, "Sincerity! Once you can fake that, you can achieve anything!" (in *Great Quotes: Vol. I, Short Quotes*, p.19). He further remarked that this quality was one MM lacked, because she could not fake sincerity.

RFK (Bobby Kennedy) had made many promises to marry MM, to lead her on, to continue their most intimate affair, an affair that involved not mere sex, but apparently MM's feelings, mind, heart and soul. MM initially believed Bobby's sincerely sounding words, and was sold hook, line, and sinker that he would marry her.

But on (or before) the 03 of August 1962 she came to the full realization that RFK had indeed lied to her, that he was insincere in his expression of feelings for her. [MLT, pp.281-284,288,290,299-300]

17.   The Loquacious Lie

To be loquacious in conversation is 'to have a rather lopsided chat, to talk chiefly about oneself as a *conversational narcissist* (coined by Charles Derber), to be given to excessive talking, non-stop, as a parliamentary pendant'.

To be a loquacious liar is 'to speak or spout incessant volumes of words (like a squid squirting black ink in the ocean) so as to hide or obscure the real message being delivered'. It's a matter of 'beating around the bush'; not cutting to the chase, the heart of the issue at hand, to be in that sense disingenuous, or obfuscating the truth.

After her last photo shoot with George Barris on 13th July 1962, MM decided to record a 42-minute reel-to-reel tape recording for her psychanalyst Ralph Greenson.

It should be noted that MM had begun to resent these loquacious and endless hours of counseling with Dr. Greenson, as she began to see them not only as fruitless, but as 'beating around the bush', disingenuous, and obfuscating the issues that needed to be discussed. She even taped 'fake monologues' and "offered them to Greenson in lieu of an agonizing session of analysis" (MLT, p.220).

18.   The Mendacious Lie

Mendacity is 'the propensity or tendency to fabricate lies, to misrepresent the true course of events, to engage regularly in falsehoods, fibs, and tall tales, to enjoy sophistry'.

For whatever reason, to this day, whenever I hear the word "mendacity" I keep hearing Burl Ives (in *The Cat on A Hot Tin Roof* movie, 1958) speaking to Paul Newman about "mendacity"!

So, this concept is quite frankly riveted in my memory, like it or not! Whenever I think of someone close to MM who exhibited this regular tendency to misrepresent both what MM said and what he said to her, and what was said about her (after her demise), I cannot help but think of Peter Lawford.

The instances of his 'mendacity' are truly too numerous to mention. He, in my overall view (having read extensively on MM's life, especially her final days), was no true friend to MM. He continually misrepresented the truth of things both to her, and about her. [MLT, pp.286-287]

To cite but one case in point (at 07:30 P.M. on the 4th of August 1962), Peter Lawford calls Marilyn to apologize for an earlier confrontation he (and RFK) had with her that afternoon. He invites her for dinner to which she declines. (MLT, p.318)

Then, according to Lawford's later testimony, MM says: "Goodbye!" to him and to tell Jack (JFK) and Bobby (RFK) that she is through with them as well, that she is through with love and all their nonsense she had to endure.

MM had distrusted Peter Lawford for a long time (not only for his cutting comments to the world when she was 'late' being strapped into her special body-clinging dress in the backroom during the JFK Birthday Gala), but because she saw that he was consistently "awfully mean" to her, for no good reason. [MLT, pp.317-318]

Even long after MM's death, Peter Lawford continued to perpetuate the myth that MM's voice over the phone to him (mere hours before her death) sounded "tired and slurred" (as if to imply that she was on a drug overdose). [MLT, p.377]

What is interesting to note, however, is that several people said that it was Peter who was thoroughly inebriated that night, and not Marilyn at all! In fact, Dr. Greenson and Joe DiMaggio, Jr. had both spoken with MM only minutes earlier, and both testified (contrary to Peter's allegations) that MM spoke clearly and distinctly.

Indeed, even Frank Sinatra felt Peter Lawford harmed MM's psyche, even to the point of blaming him for her death. (MLT, p.378)

19.   The Plagiarizing Lie

To plagiarize means 'to take the work or an idea of someone else and to pass it off as one's own'. It is a form of piracy, or counterfeiting (bootlegging, forgery), trying to take what belongs to another to imitate it as if it were one's own creation: for instance, the piracy of American movies that persists in all too many foreign countries to this day.

To plagiarize an artist, such as an actor, is to replace him or her, or his or her role or voice (as in a voice make-over in a song) with that of someone else (especially without the approval, permission, or even the knowledge of the original artist).

In MM's case, once Fox fired MM (on the grounds that she failed to appear for work when sick totaling 12 days of sick time over 32 days of shooting), they attempted to, arguably, plagiarize her role and status in the movie by contacting Kim Novak and Lee Remick to replace her (actresses whom Director George Cukor preferred to work with, it seems). [MLT, p.209]

But Dean Martin, MM's co-star, refused to go ahead with this substitution and plagiarizing of MM's title role. He bluntly stated: "No MM, No Martin!".

So, Fox promptly fired him, and all of the rest of the staff, including Cyd Charisse. Dean Martin later retaliated with a $6.8 million lawsuit against Fox for breach of contract and improper dismissal (MLT, p.246).

20. The Propagandizing Lie

Propaganda is 'a form of information especially of a biased or misleading nature (such as in a disinformation or misinformation war) used to promote or publicize a particular political cause or point of view'.

The words 'propaganda' and 'lies' in the minds of many people today are interchangeable. Perhaps its negative connotation was due to the Nazi propaganda machine of the World War II years, as well as during wartime in general?

When MM was dismissed from Fox, the rumor spread (as Fox propaganda) that it was because of her (incompetence or) failure to placate the Fox Executives that the entire staff and crew of 104 persons lost their employment as well.

This lie was especially hard-hitting for MM not only because she had never been fired before, but because she came to realize too late that she was "in the eye of a corporate hurricane," "abandoned by her erstwhile friends in the Media, and isolated by the rigors of her illness" (MLT, p.205).

To counter this propaganda-lie, MM sent a telegram (on the 11th of June 1962) to each of the 104 members of the *Something's Got to Give* set regarding their lay-offs: "It was none of my doing: I hope you know that"! [MLT, pp. 227-231]

MM feels the heat on her, and being a good sport, renegotiates the Fox contract by promoting her image, posing for various photographers from *Look* magazine, *Life* magazine, and other professional photographers all throughout June 1962, up until her final photo shoot with George Barris on the 13th of July.

21.   The Saying-White-Lies Lie

'White lies' are 'generally harmless or trivial lies, often told to avoid hurting someone's feelings' (not to be confused with 'gray lies,' 'blue lies,' 'black lies', or 'red lies'; see, *Wikipedia*).

On the 19th of May 1962 during JFK's Birthday Gala, President John F. Kennedy told (in jest) a white lie to the listening audience after MM had sung "Happy Birthday, Mr. President" (to him), that he could now retire from politics after having 'Happy Birthday!' sung to him "in such a sweet wholesome way" (MLL, p.232). Of course, everyone laughed and thought it quite amusing.

But the awful truth of the matter was that almost immediately after this Gala, the world came crashing down on MM's head. She was ostracized from the White House and told never to call JFK again. Bobby Kennedy (RFK) was sent by his elder brother to patch things up, by which was meant: To end all romantic ties with the President. Instead, it seems, RFK himself became romantically involved (as the messenger) to MM. (MLT, pp.238-239)

22. Serving-Father-Of-Lies Lie

To serve the 'father of lies' is an expression from the New Testament of the Bible, which Jesus spoke to those who opposed Him:

> Ye are of your father the devil, and the lusts of your father ye wlll do. He was a murderer from the beginning, and abode not in the truth, because there is no truth in him. When he speaketh a lie, he speaketh of his own: for he is a liar, and the father of it. (John 8:44)

On the 27-29th of July 1962, MM is 'tricked' into arriving with the Lawfords to Frank Sinatra's Cal-Neva Lodge in Lake Tahoe over that weekend. Instead of finding the comfort and respite she was seeking in Frankie's hideaway Lodge, she is introduced to Chicago crime boss, Sam Giancana, who wants more than ordinary sex with her. As one account states, Frankie simply says: "Be nice to Sam, Marilyn!" and leaves her to her own devices.

Sam Giancana (nicknamed "Momo") is fully aware that both the Kennedy brothers (JFK and RFK) have had their way with her and then dumped her. As a man who hated both the Kennedy brothers, he wishes MM to feel likewise.

And so, he sets her up for the next (and last) weekend of her life. Working on MM's emotional pain (in the way she was brushed off by the Kennedy brothers), Momo tries to break MM's spirit, to make her agree to meet with RFK that very next weekend.

But Momo, no stranger to the 'father of lies' (as recent documentaries and books on his life clearly indicate), was a full-blown psychopath (and known psychotic killer since his youth). He appeared to enjoy causing pain and displeasure to his victims.

And so, in Bungalow 52, in Frankie's Lodge, that weekend, Momo had his way with MM to bring her to that breaking point, to agree to bring RFK to her home (as Momo continually coaxed her to do), and as later events confirm.

This 'father-of-lies' lie that Momo manages to deceive MM into believing is that she had to bring RFK to her home the very next weekend. The pretext was to make RFK confess and apology to her for the way she was treated. Sadly, MM believed this 'father of all lies'.

Hence, MM became the bait Momo needed to destroy the Kennedys. With this sinister lie, and MM's unwitting compliance, the trap was set.

23.   The Stating-Whoppers Lie

Stating whoppers is 'a gross or blatantly false lie, a bold-faced, bald-faced lie. It is a sham, a yarn, a cock-and-bull story, a ruse, a myth, a pretext, a fiction that is told as a big lie, an unusually large lie, but told with a straight face'.

One of the whoppers of all lies in this study of lies (told to or about MM while she was alive) is that Bobby Kennedy never visited her during the last weekend of her life (3-4th August 1962). Yes, I realise that there is a lot of hullabaloo to the contrary, no doubt by those parties who wish to show that RFK had nothing to do with her untimely death.

And I surprisingly do agree with that point of view: JFK and RFK had no intention or desire to harm MM in any way possible.

We now 'know' (based on the detailed material supplied by the Giancana family) who killed MM, when it was done, who ordered it, what the motives apparently were, who were the other parties involved, and how the cover-up took place. All these details have now been released. [see, Part Four of this book]

But the whooper to this story is that RFK never came to visit MM in her home at all that weekend. [The narrative of events to the contrary can be found in Part Four of this book.] What is the whopper therefore is that Robert Kennedy attends Mass (at 09:30 a.m. on the 05th August 1962) at St. Mary's Roman Catholic Parish with his wife

Ethel and their 4 children in Gilroy California 79 miles south of San Francisco. He claims that he was in San Francisco for the entire weekend, and that he never visited MM's place since the 27th of June 1962 (when he went to speak to her about ending her relationship with JFK). [MLT, p.298]

But RFK was not at all surprised to hear of MM's death, we are told.

24.   The Taking-Unfair-Advantage Lie

To take an 'unfair advantage' of someone through lying is 'to be unjust, dishonest, unreasonable, improper, illegal, immoral, with undue regard for what is ethical. It involves a disproportionate or lopsided and superior competitive edge, such as in the use of loaded or false dice, to have a unique advantage or unfair lead'.

For MM, it was not fair that Fox Executives who had made 'a killing' (figuratively speaking) from her many movies she made for them would oblige her to do this 'last film' for them (which she did not wish to do). But moreover, Fox obliged MM (as their Superstar) to be paid only $100,000 to do it, a rock-bottom basement salary by any estimate.

Obviously, Fox "rescinded all of the rights and privileges [MM] had achieved after becoming a Superstar" (MLT, p.195), even though her films grossed $200 million (which is equivalent to $2 billion in 2021, according to *Wikipedia*).

Clearly, MM was taken advantage of in Fox's lie that she had no other choice but to do their bidding.

It appears MM was nothing more than a 'cash cow' to the Fox Executives. They claimed she was obliged by contract to do this one last film for them, a movie she did not wish to make, with a Director (George Cukor) who did not like her: In point of fact (as evidence now reveals), Cukor utterly loathed MM and despised her. But Fox did not seem to care about the emotional abuse (or potential harm) they caused in taking unfair advantage of their 'golden goose'.

They lied to her that she had no other choice. And to enforce that lie they apparently persuaded her 'support team' (her 'substitute family') including her own lawyer and psychoanalyst to lean on MM, to see that she would comply with their demands. (MLT, p.5)

Their 'need' of her (to complete this last film) was so fake that upon the slightest pretext (that she was sick 12 days of the 32 days scheduled for filming) they threw the book at her, fired her and threatened her with a lawsuit for $500,000!

Fox (and her own support team) clearly took unfair advantage of MM.

25.   The Untruthful Lie

To be 'untruthful' is to 'make something up, to concoct, invent, fabricate, or misrepresent things as they really are'. When someone is untruthful, they knowingly say or represent things that they know to be untrue. This form of bluffing is fraudulent and dishonest.

When MM was invited on the 17th of April 1962 to go to JFK's Birthday Gala for Saturday the 19th of May, it was an event not to be missed. She was initially informed by Fox, her employer, that she could attend. But as the weekend of the 19th of May approached, Fox changed their mind and warned MM that if she should go, she would be fired.

Both RFK and Peter Lawford reassured MM that she should go anyway, that they would "guarantee" her employment with Fox. MM left for the prestigious Gala but when she returned, Milton Gould on behalf of Fox eventually fired her. It appeared to MM that neither Peter Lawford, nor RFK, kept their word to ensure her employment with Fox.

They had been untruthful in their promise to take care of everything. (MLT, pp.133,135,169)

Part Four: The Big Lie Exposed

A.   Why the Cover-Up?

1.   What Is the Answer?

Bob Dylan in his anti-war tune has concluded that the answer to war is "Blowing in the Wind". Perhaps that is also the answer to this cover-up, the Big Lie that "MM Murdered MM"?

At any rate, this section (Part Four) will provide the running narrative (chronology of events) in the last months of Marilyn Monroe's life, to begin with December 1961, and to conclude with the final hours of her last weekend alive, as well as the immediate aftermath.

As a Testament to this cover-up (of what really happened to MM that 4th August 1962 weekend, now 60 years ago), I cite the last photographer to do a photo shoot with her (on 13th July 1962) who chatted with her over the phone on 3rd August 1962 (the day before her death), George Barris:

> The Press told the world [MM] had committed suicide. I will never believe Marilyn took her own life. She had too much to live for... She sounded so happy... It remains my belief, though I have no proof, that she was murdered. (MHOW, p.136)

I do not believe it is too late to release all the FBI and CIA files pertinent to MM's death as a full-blown murder investigation. A definitive and thorough review with all the million(s) of documents related to MM's last days on earth needs to be re-opened (MLT, p.335). Although the evidence currently available is mainly testimonial (from those who knew MM and/or who were there with her for her last weekend alive), it is not necessarily hearsay or mere rumor.

But it is, arguably, not the only evidence we currently 'have': The Classified and Secret Files of the US Security Services have the information necessary to ensure this full investigation may truly become definitive. (MLT, p.380)

Yes, expectations run high that in the year 2039 A.D. all these documents may be released as public information. But my query has not changed and still persists: "Why must we wait that long?". "What is there to hide?". Let the investigation in its full force begin. Let it begin now!

2.   The Anti-war Message

John Dylan's poignant anti-war song ("Blowing in the Wind," written in 1962) still strikes a chord 60 years later with the current War in Ukraine. It is relevant as well in our discussion of the (pending) Police State in a New World Order, a time not too far in the distant future if it has not already arrived.

I think it relevant in a world full of lies and uncertainty to reflect upon these inspiring words, which still pierce the mind and soul today of all peace-loving peoples the world over:

> How many times must the cannonballs fly
> Before they're forever banned?
> And how many years can some people exist
> Before they're allowed to be free?
> And how many ears must one man have
> Before he can hear people cry?
> Yes, and how many deaths will it take 'til he knows
> That too many people have died?

B.   MM's Last Days on Earth

1.   The Narrative: MM's Final Days

"Lies, lies, lies, nothing but lies. Everything they've been saying about me is lies!" (MM in an interview with George Barris, the last photographer to do a photo shoot with her, 13th July 1962; from *Marilyn: Her Life in Her Own Words*, George Barris, p.3.)

As so many books and articles and dozens of documentaries have been made to suggest this or that cause to be the sole reason for Ms. Monroe's untimely death, I will not dwell upon all the various points of view.

Instead, after having done extensive research on my own, and weighing the evidence so presented along with the timetable of events in the last weekend of Ms. Monroe's life, I have plotted my own conclusion, as presented by the following statements of evidence.

[The Author will reference (only some of) the remarks in the remainder of this Section from the book, *Marilyn: The Last Take*, which references will be abbreviated from henceforth as: "MLT" followed by the page number, of course.]

It is my understanding that commencing on 1st January 2039, UCLA (The University of California in Los Angeles) will provide an official release of all documents and private recordings held previously by Marilyn Monroe's psychiatrist, Dr. Ralph Greenson, to the public at large. (See, Notes of Explanation, #13.)

There will also be (it is expected at that time if not sooner) a full release of all (redacted and unredacted) files currently held by the CIA and FBI on Marilyn Monroe's life and death, in particular her complete unredacted phone log on that fateful last weekend of her life. [Missing telephone records are located in FBI File 66-1700-39, according to Jack Clemmons, Robert Slatzer, and Anthony Summers. (MLT, p.410)]

[I understand that Anthony Summers, author of *Goddess: The Secret Lives of Marilyn Monroe*, was able to obtain a partially declassified or unredacted phone log of Marilyn Monroe's last weekend calls after nine years of solicitation. (MLT, 354)]

Therefore, this current exercise in this book will be at best a precursor to the eventual full release of all of these documents and accumulated evidence heretofore held by the departments and agencies so expressed. "Why do you not simply wait to see what the full story of Ms. Monroe's death will entail in seventeen years?" one may ask.

Well, simply put, because there has been a truly significant outpouring of details pertaining to her demise (to date) so much so that I do believe my current point of view will be largely (if not fully) substantiated by these future revelations (in 2039). In other words, I doubt that there is a need to wait another seventeen years to see what actually transpired during those last three days of her life (3rd to 5th August 1962).

What is disconcerting to me is that the detailed phone log of Ms. Monroe is still being detained and withheld (redacted) by the CIA and FBI who (as we shall see) were apparently involved in her untimely death. (MLT, pp.325-327,373-374)

Opponents to the status quo will hastily label this 'theory' (or any other theory) as a 'conspiracy theory' which to do so is to throw mud onto the evidence thus far accumulated.

We need to have an open mind and no pre-conceived notions as to Marilyn Monroe's cause of death in order to discover the true course of events, as well as the true nature of her death. Anyone can concoct any kind of tale (or absurdity) as they wish, but the genuine lovers of truth will stick to the facts of the case as we now know them to be.

Many thanks of course to the peers and relations of those persons involved in Marilyn Monroe's life, as well as those who knew her personally, for their testimonials and assistance in creating this timeline leading up to her death.

2.   December 1961

Marilyn Monroe was told on 16th December by Fox that she had to complete one more film entitled: *"Something's Got to Give"* in order to be released from her movie contract. She tried to refuse to make any more movies with Fox (especially after her disastrous relationship with Director George Cukor in *Let's Make Love,* shot in 1960).

But her lawyer Milton Rudin advised MM that she had no choice, legally speaking. Even her Swiss-trained psychoanalyst, Ralph Greenson, persuaded MM that she should 'work for her emotional health' (MLT, p.44).

To make matters even worse, the openly Gay Director (dubbed "the Little Dictator"; MLT, pp. 32,53,111,119), George Cukor, was ordered by Fox to work as Director for MM in *"Something's Got to Give"*, also his final legally binding commitment to Fox (MLT, p.51).

As the following months (in 1962) would reveal, Cukor loathed and even downright hated MM with an unrelenting passion (because as rumors still have it, he was snubbed by bi-sexual Yves Montand in *Let's Make Love,* who clung onto MM instead; MLT, pp. 28-33,60,114-116).

Cukor who had MM perform dozens of (now believed to have been) utterly senseless yet painstaking re-takes (in an attempt to demoralize her apparently) made a written request to Fox (on 6th June 1962) to have MM fired which Fox did on 8th June 1962 (MLT, pp. 52,199).

As Cukor put it: 'She [MM] is a spoiled, pampered Superstar and represents all that is bad about Hollywood today". (MLT, p.52) Cukor's (not so secret) wish to 'derail' *Something's Got to Give* finally brought down the curtain with MM's (arguably) unjustified dismissal (MLT, p.175-177).

Thereafter, MM's personal life for several reasons also begins to spiral downwards. But I'm ahead of this (tragic) tale.

MM attends a Christmas party hosted by Patricia Kennedy Lawford at the Lawford Beach Mansion where she meets Jack Kennedy (JFK). Private detective Fred Otash later testifies that his 'bugs' in the Lawford Mansion "picked up the steamy love scene between politician [JFK] and movie star [MM] during the posh Christmas party" (MLT, p. 71).

So began the fatal attraction between the world's 'sexiest' movie star and the world's 'sexiest' politician (as RFJ would later describe it) (MLT, p.133).

3.   January 1962

This New Year was the turning point for MM. She wanted finally to own her own house. With ex-hubby Joe DiMaggio's timely aid, she purchased a lovely hacienda-style home (listed for $77,500) for only $52,500. [This hacienda remained unsold after MM's untimely death until 2017 when it sold in ten days for $7.25 million.]

MM was so elated about her new home (at 12-305 and Fifth Helena Drive, in Brentwood, Los Angeles 49, California) that she exclaimed to her masseur, Ralph Roberts: "I have finally arrived in a point of my life in which I am truly happy. It's so good to finally own my own home! I feel like laughing again! It feels so good!".

Ironically, MM's new home had the motto *Cursum Perificio* written into The Coat of Arms (in the pavement entrance) which translated means: "My Journey ends here!".

4.   February 1962

MM flies to Mexico City on the 10th of February (for ten days) to meet with several people including ex-hubby Joe DiMaggio (who hints at remarriage but does not formally propose). MM's main goal in Mexico City is to look to buy Mexican-style furniture for her newly acquired hacienda, which is being custom-built to MM's specifications (MLT, p.61).

She apparently prepays for a distinctive sofa which does not arrive at her home until 04th August, the last day of her life. [The sofa remains in its original shipping crate until it is 'sold as is' in Christie's Auction in 1999.]

On 27th February 1962, J. Edgar Hoover (head of the FBI) notifies Bobby Kennedy (RFK) that the FBI discovered JFK had an intimate affair with Judith Campbell Exner, "a sometimes mistress of Sam Giancana, the Chicago crime boss.

The implication is that Frank Sinatra had 'fixed Kennedy up' with Campbell (MLT, p.167). Although Sinatra spent $1.2 million to enhance his Lake Tahoe hideaway (the Cal-Nev Lodge) anticipating a JFK visit thereafter, JFK's political advisors declares Sinatra as "an undesirable person". He is therewith dropped by JFK and completely ostracized from the White House on 28th February 1962.

As Giancana would occasionally stay at the Cal-Nev Lodge (being part-owner), it became too dangerous politically for JFK to be seen there. In only three months, Sinatra would be giving the same (hard) advice to MM, that the Kennedy's would be dropping her (as they did him), and that she would likewise become ostracized.

5.   March 1962

MM begins to undertake a few renovations. She has plans to redo the landscaping of her hacienda. Inside the walls surrounding her home (which were two feet thick and seven feet high) was a secret garden. "Hillocks of baby's breath and veins of German moss stretched along a flagstone walkway. Brilliant bougainvillea vines made crimson splashes against white-washed walls" (MLT, p.273).

Already early in the year, MM adds "flowering bushes, Oriental bulbs, and sweet olive trees" (MLT, p.273). She wants to add her 'personal stamp' to her 'secret garden'. Eunice Murray, MM's housekeeper, gives Marilyn a gift, a book on horticulture, which can be seen on MM's night-table (next to her bed) the day of her death.

As MM needs to re-wire the house, she is approached by several different persons: Bernard Spindall (formerly from the Military Signal Corps), and Fred Kotash, among others, who apparently offer MM a deal too good to refuse. (MLT, p.71)

But as it turns out, these men are professional conmen who wiretap and bug MM's home to include orders from: (1) J. Edgar Hoover (of the FBI); (2) The CIA; (3) Jimmy Hoffa (of the Teamsters' Union); and (4) Sam Giancana, a Chicago Mafia boss. (MLT, pp. 254,308-309,410).

Their motives are simply to tape-record all the phone calls and activities that MM undergoes, especially with her liaisons with the Kennedy brothers, JFK (John Fitzgerald Kennedy, the 35th US President); and RFK (Robert Francis Kennedy, the 64th US Attorney General).

In later months, MM becomes suspicious that people are listening on her line (due to 'clicks' she hears), and so she begins to call (whenever convenient) from a nearby payphone. Peter Lawford's beach home (located at 625 Pacific Coast Highway in Santa Monica) not far from MM's home is also bugged and wiretapped by the CIA and FBI (MLT, p.71).

This beach home becomes the rendezvous for RFK later in June and July of this year. It consists of 27 rooms (14 of which are bedrooms and hidden suites), along with a heated marble pool (MLT, pp. 252-253).

[The excuses later made by these Security Agencies is that it was necessary to bug and wiretap all the various homes of JFK's lovers as he would repeatedly 'duck' from these Secret Service Agents to rendezvous with his 'sweethearts'. Because of political tensions with Cuba at the time, it was imperative that the 'nuclear football' suitcase be close at hand to JFK at all times.

In plain language, the Security protecting the President had to know where he was at all times. In addition, J. Edgar Hoover (head of the FBI) had created a file for MM as a potential Communist agent, as she had defended her ex-husband Arthur Miller (whom Joe McCarthy had accused of attending Communist rallies in the 1940s).

The Monday after MM's death (the 6th August 1962) it is reported that J. Edgar Hoover declared that a victory against Communism had been achieved.]

MM receives a Golden Globe Award this month (for several film roles including) for her role in *The Misfits* (Arthur Miller's 'Valentine' to MM). MM had completed the film in Nevada in October 1960 but had to re-do the ending with Clark Gable in the Studio in November of that year.

Two days after completing the final take, Clark Gable has a heart attack and dies 16th of November 1960, leaving MM so devastated that she couldn't seem to function normally, nor work throughout 1961.

To console MM, Frank Sinatra gives her a white terrier which she names "Mafia Honey" (or Maf, for short) because of Frankie's purported connections to the Mafia. (Marilyn's sense of humour). [The two original Polaroid photos MM had of Maf sold in Christie's Auction in 1999 for $100,000 each.]

6.   April 1962

On 8th April, MM is to begin to work for Fox (under the basement bottom price of only $100,000) along with Dean Martin, her co-star (who is paid $500,000). But the Director, George Cukor, didn't like the script. And so, it all had to be rewritten. Production would have to be delayed until the 23rd of April. (MLT, p.66)

On the 17th of April, MM receives an official invitation from the White House to attend JFK's 45th Birthday Gala held jointly at the Democratic National Convention on Saturday, 19th of May. Fox initially replies (though not officially) that MM could go to Madison Square Garden for the Gala celebration.

[Later, Milton S. Gould (who ran Fox at the time) reversed that decision and demanded MM work even on Saturdays (to include the 19th of May); MLT, p.233.]

But MM listens to RFK who reassures her that he will take care of Fox for her. (MLT, pp.129,132-135) MM goes ahead and orders a special dress for the occasion, which would increase in price from $5,000 to $12,000 (MLT, pp.133,392). [This Jean Louis dress would later sell in November 2016 at Julien's Auction for $4.81 million, the most expensive dress in recorded history! (MLT, pp.136-141)]

MM could now phone directly to the Oval Office and speak directly to JFK's secretary, Evelyn Lincoln, to arrange a rendezvous with "Jack" wherever he wished: the Carlyle Hotel, the Lawford Mansion, the Beverly Hilton Hotel, or even aboard Air Force One. "When the President beckoned, Marilyn responded" (MLT, pp.68-74).

MM's trip therefore on the 18th of April to pick up her drama coach, Paula Strasberg, was actually (in part) a cover to meet with 'Jack' (JFK) (MLT, pp. 74-75) But MM's trip to NYC to visit her mentor, Lee Strasberg, ensured she caught his viral cold just as MM had to return to L.A. to continue her work (MLT, pp.74-75).

7.   May 1962

Having returned from NYC to LA on 19th April 1962, MM became quite ill by the 20th of April. Filming for *Something's Got to Give* was to commence on Monday, 23rd April 1962; but by Sunday, the 22nd of April, MM was dangerously ill and had to be rushed to Cedars of Lebanon Hospital for 2 p.m. Tests there confirmed that MM's acute viral cold from a few days ago "had developed into a massive sinus infection":

> She suffered high fevers [of 101 degrees] and diz-ziness, unbearable headaches, and lethargy. The tests also showed that she had contracted the most severe form of the disease, 'chronic sinusitis,' which usually required a month of massive antibi-otic treatment to cure" (MLT, pp.76-79).

Lee Siegel, Fox Studio's physician (who had treated MM since 1951) recommended that MM be given a month's rest.

But Fox Executives (especially Phil Feldman) refused to accept that request, stating (privately) that as this was MM's last film with the Studio that she should be given 'hot shots' to artificially shock her back into health. The attitude of Fox Executives (as related by MM's physician Lee Siegel) was (to quote them verbatim): "Let Marilyn collapse after we finish"! (MLT, p.81)

(This treatment was not uncommon in Hollywood Studios having been used with marked success particularly with racehorses when the stakes are high and the horse's life after the race is of no consequence to its owners.)

For MM, therefore, she would be given these 'hot shots' twice daily to perk her up and have her back to work in no time. MM had been given these injections previously during the filming of *The Misfits* when Arthur Miller insisted MM finish that filming in the hot Arizona desert ASAP.

As Dr. Siegel described their composition: "They contained methamphetamines, a few vitamins glucose to give an immediate lift, and a small amount of Librium to smooth out the effect of the uppers" (MLT, pp.81-82). These man-made chemical pills were merely another tool to keep MM working far beyond her normal body tolerance (MLT, pp.83-84).

Given these semi-daily 'hot shot' injections, MM was able to come onto the Studio set briefly on 30th April, fainted on 1st May, then worked 9 hours straight on 7th May, suffering a relapse on 8th May, and therefore being forced to confinement until the 14th May (MLT, p.112).

The irony was that although MM was ready to go at it, back to work in full swing on the 14th May, no one else in the Studio, especially the Director George Cukor was up to it. The previous three months of a virtual total standstill (as MM was in almost every scene) resulted in a demoralizing resentment to MM (MLT, p.104).

To make matters even worse, MM was scheduled to leave Friday the 18th to rehearse in NYC for the Presidential Gala on Saturday the 19th. Fox Studio intervened and demanded MM not leave for the Gala, having rescinded their previous permission allowing her to leave, on pain of being fired. Bobby Kennedy, however, reassured MM that he would take care of everything (MLT, pp. 132-135).

Fox Studio was upset that MM's three weeks off work cost them almost $100,000 in production costs (as they had 104 employees on the set). What Fox did not disclose however was that MM's chief Fox rival, Elizabeth Taylor (the 'world's most famous femme fatale', MLT, p.90) had cost Fox Executives $8,000,000 (that's eight million dollars!) due to her "bouts of pneumonia and bronchitis" which delayed the production of *Cleopatra* for seven months! (MLT, p.78)

The intimate relationship between MM and JFK (having met six times before May) came to a climax on 19th May for MM's 'swan song' as she sings "Happy Birthday, Mr. President" to JFK. A jubilant Bobby Kennedy had arranged this entire spoof for his elder brother JFK.

But many people simply felt that MM's appearance at Madison Square Garden "would be like Marilyn making love to the President publicly after doing it privately all these months" (MLT, p.70).

Joseph Kennedy, JFK and RFK's father (who had suffered a stroke in December 1961 and), who wanted his son, JFK, to run for re-election in 1963, put his foot down demanding JFK end his liaisons with MM (which RFK as the dutiful brother was ordered to perform). [MLT, p.289]

To appease Fox Studio Productions, MM did a nude swimming scene on 23rd May after 5 p.m. which still photographs "eventually appeared on the covers of seventy-two magazines in thirty-two countries--some of them behind the Iron Curtain" (MLT, pp.156-161).

But her plan did not work! Fox was not pleased with MM's 'swan song' to JFK. RFK and Peter Lawford had lied to her. They did not guarantee her job with Fox as they promised they would (MLT, pp.132-135,169,189,191).

To make matters even worse, it appeared that JFK had just used her, and now intended to throw her away. MM could see herself now as a world-wide joke, nothing more than a high-class call-girl at best. As of 25th May, all her calls to the White House were disconnected. JFK had cut her off completely.

But according to one of MM's closest actress friends, Terry Moore, Bobby Kennedy "had been delegated to put an end to the affair" (MLT, pp.168-169). Bobby (RFK) was, after all, the family's "sexual policeman" for both John and Teddy Kennedy (MLT, p.253).

Just as Cleopatra of old awaited the arrival of Mark Antony who was delegated by Rome to discipline her, to put her in her place, so MM looked forward to the arrival of RFK. (RFK had, after all, insisted to dance five times with MM the evening of the Gala "while an angry Ethel Kennedy looked on" MLT, p.150-151).

Between 21 May and 1st June, MM worked nine days and completed ten key scenes, while she was 'emotionally shattered. "Her appearance at the Gala now promised to destroy her career. And, in repayment, the First Family had cut her adrift" (MLT, p.169).

As Frank Sinatra confirmed with MM (via phone) on 26-27th May, JFK was through with her. MM disappeared for those two days but returned to work on 28th May, Monday. It was rumoured she might have had a "clandestine abortion" (MLT, p.166).

8.   June 1962

On 1st June, MM turned 36 years old, a pivotal age for an actress. Clara Bow, Joan Crawford, Greta Garbo, and Gloria Swanson all were considered 'box-office poison' when they turned thirty-six (although actresses, such as Joan Crawford, did make a comeback in later years) (MLT, p.173-174).

Yet when Jane Fonda shared with MM her wish once all the youthful 'vapid sex symbol' is gone, an actress could then finally "begin to play character roles and rely on acting alone," MM expressed a "despair akin to that of a painter who discovers that he is going blind, or of a pianist whose hands are becoming arthritic" (MLT, p.174,178-179).

For Elizabeth Taylor's 30th birthday in February 1962, Fox spent almost $5,000 but for MM's 36th birthday MM's stand-in, Evelyn Moriarty, bought her a "five-dollar sheet cake", and Fox only bought her a large urn of coffee (from the Fox snack bar), but they later billed it back to MM's estate (after she died).

Marilyn could feel all of their bad vibes. She was denied all the prerogatives of a Star (MLT, p.116). She was not allowed time off for her birthday until after 6 p.m. as if she were 'a bad child' (MLT, pp.176-177).

So, MM has a very low-key birthday party at her home late in the evening, with Dean Martin present, Director George Cukor, and a few photographers. Her home is still under renovation and appears quite empty of furniture (as she is still awaiting the custom-built furniture from Mexico). But everyone makes the best of it.

Unbeknown to MM, Fox had planned to fire her on the 8th of June, the same day they intended to fire Elizabeth Taylor but for a lot more reasons (MLT, p.182,202). Liz Taylor's living expenses alone reached $228,000 (more than double MM's entire salary for *Something's Got to Give*).

Taylor's overtime rates (at $10,000 per day) along with 10% of the gross (whether or not the film turned a profit), and her insistence that *Cleopatra* be filmed in Todd-A-O, "the wide-screen process created by her late husband, Michael Todd" ensured that her initial $1,000,000 salary more than double to a final profit (to include royalties, etc.) estimated to be: $7,000,000! (MLT, pp.91-95)

Yet more important than these financial losses incurred by incessant delays due to Liz Taylor's delicate health (for which no Insurance Company would ensure her as an employee of Fox since her near-death in March 1961 which required a tracheotomy; MLT, p. 92), was the very public very open love affair between Liz Taylor and Richard Burton while Burton was still married to Sybil, and Taylor to Eddie Fisher (MLT, pp. 366-367).

They were referred to as "The Hollywood Jezebel and her Welsh gigolo' (MLT, p.367). The USA refused them entry; and Italy (prompted by the Vatican) condemned Liz Taylor as "an undesirable person" (MLT, pp.124-128). To add insult to injury, Richard Burton on full salary had "worked only five times in the first seventeen weeks, and only thirty days in the entire first year" (MLT, p.97).

But Liz Taylor threatened to sue Fox and to "tie up the film [*Cleopatra*] for years" if she were fired [MLT, p.187]. Her ruse worked. The Fox Executives "couldn't get rid of Taylor, so they decided to show they were strong men and fired Monroe--in Taylor's place" (MLT, p.205).

But MM was "cushioned by a false sense of security". "Abandoned by her erstwhile friends in the media, and isolated by the rigours of her illness, Monroe was in the eye of a corporate hurricane" (MLT, p.205).

MM had no idea that Fox was really going to fire her until "the studio shut down production without even informing her" on the 6th of June (MLT, p.206). MM (who had previously believed filming would resume on the 11th of June) was devastated when she was told by her own psychoanalyst, Ralph Greenson, on the 8th of June that she was fired. MM had never been fired before.

She felt betrayed by her own support group, which 'substitute family' (she concluded) had "done more harm than good" on her behalf (MLT, p. 206, 277). She felt that she should dismiss all the following 'family members' from her payroll (as they did not properly protect her from being fired by Fox): Pat Newcomb (her so-called publicist); Paula Strasberg (her drama coach, whom MM was paying $3,000/week); Ralph Greenson, who MM was paying $1400/month (MLT, pp. 220,228); Eunice Murray (her so-called housemaid hired by Dr. Greenson, but who was secretly a psychiatric nurse collecting data on MM), and the list goes on (MLT, pp. 205-207, 241-242).

But the worse was yet to come: Fox set out to destroy MM's reputation as a superstar. "The publicists dredged up two of Marilyn's most private heartbreaks: her fear of insanity, and her long-hidden history of learning disabilities. Cleverly and insidiously, they turned these faults into a firestorm." (MLT, p. 219). They campaign to "Get Marilyn" headed by Herry Brand. (MLT, pp. 210-211,398)

Even George Cukor, MM's director, wrote to Fox that MM "the poor dear has finally gone around the bend" (p.217). Monroe was depicted as 'half-mad' (MLT, p. 211). Then the knock-out punch came from Fox's own Chief of Production, Peter G. Levathes, to *The Times* that: "Miss Monroe is not just being temperamental; she is mentally ill, perhaps seriously" (MLT, p. 215).

On the 8th of June, Levathes directs Frank Ferguson, Fox's top lawyer, to officially fire MM ("one of the most financially successful stars in Fox's history"; MLT, p. 190), and to charge her with a $500,000 lawsuit on the grounds that she violated her Fox Contract and did not show up for work when required to do so. They try to replace her with Kim Novak or Lee Remick.

But Dean Martin (MM's co-star) insists on the exact wording of the Fox Contract. He thereby refuses to work with anyone but MM, stating: "No MM, No Martin!" (MLT, pp. 224-225). So, Fox dutifully fires Dean Martin and all the rest of the staff, including Cyd Charisse. Dean Martin later retaliates on the 24th of June with a $6.8 million lawsuit against Fox (MLT, p. 246).

Marilyn truly appreciates the loyalty of Dean Martin; and sends a telegram to each of the 104 cast and crew members who were all laid off (on the 11th June) to say to each one of them regarding their lay-offs: "It was none of my doing: I hope you know that"! (MLT, pp. 227-231)

MM feels the heat on her, and being a good sport, renegotiates the Fox Contract by promoting her image, posing for various photographers from *Look* magazine, *Life* magazine, and other professional photographers all throughout June, and up until the 13th July.

9.   Summer of Love

Since the first week of June, Marilyn (MM) & Bobby (RFK) became an item. Their initial contact (following the magic chemistry in the post-Gala evening celebration of JFK's birthday on 19th May 1962) was in MM's garden. MM's maid (Hazel Washington who viewed the 'courtship') compared it to "making love over the phone. And I do mean 'making love'"! (MLT, p. 253)

MM and RFK became "soulmates, from the beginning" (MLT, p. 251) as their places of rendezvous varied from the Presidential Suite at the Beverly Hilton in LA, MM's apartment in Hollywood, MM's own Brentwood hacienda, and the Lawford's Mansion in Santa Monica.

The Lawford neighbours, Lynn Sherman and Peter Dye, not only saw Bobby and Marilyn spending the weekend of

23-24 June 1962 walking together along the Santa Monica beach but were both "convinced that overnight trysts were involved" (MLT, p. 254).

Detectives working for the Mafia and who had bugged the Lawford Beach Home could attest to the many 'on-again, off-again' affairs in their love nests (MLT, p. 254) [See also, FBI File 66-1700-39; MLT, p. 410]. MM was "absolutely starstruck" with RFK, sharing her "far from sexless" intimate evenings with Bobby "repeatedly during June and July 1962]" (MLT, pp. 252-259).

These sexual encounters were well known by many persons in MM's inner circle, News reporters, researchers, and local politicians including the following: (1) Ralph Roberts; (2) LA Mayor Sam Yorty; (3) James Spada (Peter Lawford's biographer); (4) Anthony Summers; (5) Mike Carroll (LA Deputy District Attorney); (6) Hazel Washington (MM's personal assistant); (7) Gene Allen; (8) Natalie Jacobs; (9) Rupert Allan; (10) Pat Newcomb; (11) Dorris Johnson; (12) Dorothy Manners; (13) Ed Guthman; (14) Robert Slatzer (MM's masseur); (15) Terry Moore (actress); (16) James Bacon (Journalist); (17) Eunice Murray (MM's housekeeper); (18) Jeanne Carmen (MM's confidante), and others (MLT, p.386). MM was of the belief that "Sex isn't wrong if there's love in it"! (MLT, p. 260).

MM's seemingly endless 'summer of love' was shortly to come to a brutal finale. As with the true story of Mark Antony who was sent (by the Roman Emperor Octavian) to rule over Egypt, but who became seduced instead by the Egyptian Queen Cleopatra, so Bobby Kennedy was sent by his brother Jack to discipline (or control) Marilyn, to break off all relations between MM and JFK. (MLT, p. 289)

But instead, RFK became embroiled in an intimate ongoing love tryst with MM (MLT, p. 286). And as Mark Antony was already married to Octavian's sister, Octavia, but continued the affair with Cleopatra, so Bobby (Kennedy) who was married to Ethel (Kennedy) apparently followed suit. The key difference was that only MM died not long after her love affair with Bobby, whereas both Cleopatra and Mark Antony committed suicide.

Meanwhile, on the other side of the world, in Rome, Elizabeth Taylor and Richard Burton who were supposed to only 'pretend' as actors (and as a publicity stunt to advertise the movie *Cleopatra*) to be passionately in love (playing the roles of Cleopatra and Mark Antony, respectively) actually became sexual lovers on and off the screen (although both persons were married to other spouses).

Indeed, Liz Taylor, in particular, seemed to have rehearsed this role (as a home breaker; MLT, p. 90) with her then-current husband, Eddie Fisher. After the tragic death of Liz Taylor's third husband (Michael Todd), Liz's 'best friend', Debbie Reynolds, sent her husband, Eddie Fisher, to 'console Liz'. Elizabeth instead (as the story goes) seduced Eddie Fisher, had him divorce his wife, Debbie Reynolds, and marry her (MLT, p. 389). Then, not long thereafter (during the filming of *Cleopatra*) Taylor repeatedly seduced Richard Burton off-screen (as was her part, or role, in the movie on-screen) much to the chagrin of the movie moguls.

10.   July 1962

MM had lost 27 pounds for her last contractual obligation with Fox, *Something's Got to Give*. And as the many photo-shoots (of June and July 1962) and the many out-takes from that final film still clearly indicate: She never looked better, perhaps even ten years younger! (MLT, pp. 36-37,114-115, 274).

In compliance with the demands of Fox to become reinstated with a new contract, MM had to dismiss her entourage of 'consultants', to include: Pat Newcomb, Paula Strasberg, Dr. Ralph Greenson, Eunice Murray, and so forth (MLT, pp. 203, 206-207, 241-242, 277-278, 293-294).

Perhaps it is for this reason that MM (after her last photo-shoot of 13th July) decided to record a 42-minute reel-to-reel tape recording for her psychoanalyst, Ralph Greenson? It has been noted that MM had begun to resent these endless hours of counselling with Dr. Greenson, as she began to see them as totally fruitless. She even taped 'fake monologues' and "offered them to Greenson in lieu of an agonizing session of analysis" (MLT, p. 220).

On this final recording she ever made (for Dr. Greenson) she declared that she was finally free of all her past hangups, that she felt she no longer needed his services, that she was free of all her past love trysts, that she found happiness to simply go on with her life, to live her own career, and to be free and single as she is now (according to John Miner's notes from this tape to which Dr. Greenson had allowed him to listen).

This final recording is to be released, declassified, to the public on 1st January 2039 (together with all other collected materials in Box 39, to contain correspondence, letters, and notes in the Special Collections located at UCLA, as set up by the late Dr. Greenson. Greenson had played this final recording for John Miner before he, Dr. Greenson, died (on 24 November 1979). [See, Notes of Explanation, #13.]

Apparently, this final recording contained rather intimate and personal comments MM made to Greenson, which comments Greenson asked John Miner not to disclose to the public. Miner felt after Greenson's death that he could relay at least the less intimate details on that recording.

The one detail of note that Miner released was the final verbatim quote MM had read into her last taped recording that pertained to Bobby Kennedy. MM purportedly disclosed the following personal confession: "As you see, there is no room in my life for him (RFK). I guess I don't have the courage to face up to it and hurt him. I want someone else to tell him it's over! I tried to get the President to do it, but I couldn't reach him." (*Wikipedia*, "John Miner")

Miner did say that having listened to this tape made only two weeks prior to MM's death, that there is no possible way she would have wanted to commit suicide.

MM believed simply that "A girl doesn't need anyone who doesn't need her!". And so, with the gnawing and growing realization that both the Kennedy brothers were simply using her, and that they would drop her "once they got what they wanted" (MLT, p. 265), she decided to be the one to leave first. As MM said before: "A wise girl kisses but doesn't love, listens but doesn't believe, and leaves before she is left"!

But sometime in mid-July, MM discovers that she is pregnant for approximately one month (during her period). Doing the math in reverse, she realizes that it could only be RFK's baby (MLT, pp. 282-284). As MM wanted to do the right thing: To quietly have another 'clandestine abortion' (she had six previously along with four miscarriages; MLT, p. 103), she thought she should at the very least let Bobby know that she was 'in the way'.

As MM wanted one last encounter with Bobby Kennedy (possibly to simply state that she was pregnant with his child and wanted to see if he objected to an abortion as he was Catholic), to her amazement when she called the White House, she was told emphatically not to call anymore, neither for JFK, nor for RFK!

MM believed that "we all have insecurities of one kind and another, but it's hardly an excuse for bad manners or bad behaviour". She knew that JFK was sexually prolific, that he had many sex partners, and that she was only one pebble among many on the beach (MLT, pp. 73-74).

But to sing: 'Happy Birthday, Mr. President' was an honor so high, so desirable that it is said Marilyn would have "come back from the dead" to sing it! (MLT, p.144)

Picture this scenario, as Henry Weinstein points out:

> Here's a girl who really did come from the streets, who had a mother who wasn't all there; and a father who had disappeared; a girl who had known all the poverty in the world. And now she was going to sing 'Happy Birthday' to the President of the United States in Madison Square Garden. There was no way for her to resist that! (MLT, p. 135).

MM eventually realized that neither of the Kennedy brothers would leave his spouse to marry her. As in the movie created in that same year, *Love with The Proper Stranger*, there is a fair amount of stress for a woman to go through an abortion because of unrequited love, a lop-sided love, a love that is not returned.

MM simply wanted a 'Goodbye kiss', to be let down gently, with respect, with a sense of admiration she (falsely) assumed the Kennedy brothers had for her. She could "never understand why the President, and later the Attorney General, hadn't the courage or the gallantry to tell her 'Goodbye' themselves" (MLT, p. 278).

Bobby Kennedy ended Monroe's 'bittersweet romance' in a "particularly brutal manner": "He did it cruelly, like a rich college boy dumping a girlfriend from the wrong side of the tracks. She had been fun; she had been exciting. But she was used up." Bobby's heartless dismissal of MM was "a macho act of a sort highly regarded within the Kennedy clan". (MLT, pp. 264-265)

As Patricia Seaton Lawford describes it: "It seems as though Joe Kennedy's children, and the men and women they married, have a history of emotional and physical abuse. The men have a tendency to use women sexually and then discard them. This masks their own ability to feel." (MLT, p. 266) According to Pat Seaton Lawford (in her conversation with MM about 'Bobby's false promises'): "Bobby's still a little boy wanting to play like a little boy!" (MLT, p. 281)

But MM couldn't simply let the lost love affair come to an end as a 'silent treatment' from both the Kennedy brothers, without the courtesy of an explanation. She felt used, abused, and discarded as a lemon sucked dry, as an object of lust, not as a friend or former confidante. She had wanted to end the affair herself in a gentlemanly and polite way. Not like this, not to be dropped like a hot potato, to be treated like a tramp, as a saloon girl (MLT, pp.18, 255,264-265).

So, after contacting her former gynecologist, Leon Khron, on 19th July 1962, MM went incognito (under an assumed name) into Cedars of Lebanon Hospital for a 'quickie abortion'. She returned home on the evening of 21ˢᵗ July 1962. (MLT, pp. 282-283).

MM then called Bobby Kennedy (between 22-26 July 1962) at his home in Hickory Hill in Arlington, Virginia having obtained his personal phone number from movie producer Jerry Wald (who was working on Bobby's film, *The Enemy Within*). Bobby who was trying to distance himself completely from MM was "furious with Marilyn for taking this liberty" (MLT, p. 280).

11.   27-29 July 1962: Cal-Neva

RFK then requests Peter Lawford to ensure that MM was out of LA for the weekend of 27-29ᵗʰ July 1962 as he plans to be there for several public appearances. Peter of course complies and arranges matters for MM letting her believe that Frank Sinatra wants to be with her in Lake Tahoe at his "Cal-Neva" Lodge (named after the fact that it is located on the California-Nevada border). Reports state that Peter Lawford gives MM an abundance of drugs to prepare her for her arrival at the Lodge, as if he tried to drug her. (MLT, p.286)

As MM still carries a torch for Sinatra (who had given her a pair of emerald earrings last Summer), she thinks perhaps Frankie is thinking to propose. But MM is to suddenly learn upon arrival that Frankie ('Blue Eyes') is actually now engaged to dancer Juliet Prowse! (MLT, pp. 285-286,289)

Instead of finding comfort and understanding in Frankie's 'hideaway' Lodge, MM meets Chicago Crime Boss, Sam Giancana, who wants more than ordinary sex with her. As one account states, Frankie simply says: "Be nice to Sam, Marilyn!" and leaves her to her own devices.

What followed is detailed in various commentaries and biographies on Marilyn, but noteworthy in Daniel Bates' exposé: "Marilyn spent her last night with Mafia boss at Frank Sinatra's Lodge" (in *Lexis Nexis Academic*, 29 April 2011).

Marilyn was fully aware of the lust many men had for her, as she adeptly describes (as a 'changeable nature') in these lyrics of a song ("After you Get What you Want") she once sang:

> There's a longing in your eye, hard to satisfy And here's the reason why: 'Cause after you get what you want, you don't want it. You're like a baby: you want what you want when you want it; but after you are presented with what you want, you're discontented!

As Leonard Cohen in one of his esoterical ballads ("Take This Longing") describes this romantic side of yearning for a beautiful woman:

> Everyone who wanted you. They found what they will always want again. Your beauty lost to you yourself. Just as it was lost to them. Oh, take this longing from my tongue. Whatever useless things

these hands have done. Let me see your beauty broken down. Like you would do for one you love!

Although MM knew she had "flesh appeal" or "flesh impact" (MLT, p. 19-20), she began to lament this image, this 'sex symbol', she had become: It clearly affected her personal life, with those men she thought cared for her. She saw (too late) that because her body 'turned men on', she became "a failure as a woman", as she explains:

> My men expect so much of me, because of the image they've made of me—and that I've made of myself—as a sex symbol. They expect so much, and I can't live up to it. They expect bells to ring and whistles to whistle, but my anatomy is the same as any other woman's and I can't live up to it. (MLT, p.260)

Marilyn eventually saw the destructive result of this 'image' of herself in her relations with JFK, which she did not at first realise, as one commentator put it: "Marilyn didn't realize that JFK wasn't interested in having sex with Marilyn Monroe: He wanted to have sex with the greatest movie star of the day. She was just a symbol to him. Nothing more." (MLT, p.74)

The key problem with this encounter with (the much older) Sam "Momo" Giancana was that there was no soft romance here, no intention to 'be nice' to Marilyn, but only the one component: to break Marilyn's spirit, to have her agree to meet with RFK, to threaten to expose the Kennedy affair, so that Sam could exact his revenge on these two men whom he despised and hated above all others.

To ensure Marilyn's cooperation, Sam degrades her (in Bungalow 52) in front of photographers who take a total of 14 instant Polaroid photos [with Frank Sinatra's own new camera (which just came out into the market the previous year)].

Marilyn was apparently used as a plaything by Sam Giancana to the point that she couldn't pop pills, drink enough champagne, and force herself into a semi-comatose state fast enough. Sam Giancana (a known psychopath since his early youth, according to the documentary, *Momo*) in his hatred for the Kennedy brothers sets MM up for the last weekend of her life.

Momo's contract (to eliminate MM) was preconditioned on the taped evidence of RFK in MM's fully-bugged bungalow. [The plan (as several sources indicate) was to use MM as a foil, as bait, in order to incriminate RFK for MM's murder (which murder was set to take place after RFK leaves MM's home).

But things did not go exactly as planned by these cold-blooded killers, as we shall see.]

One could only imagine what may have occurred, although leaked reports indicate that *La Dolce Vita* (an Italian 1960 movie that mimicked the sex-suicide culture of the idle rich) captured the mood in that Lodge that Saturday night.

On this day, Saturday, the 28th of July 1962 (the last day of filming for *Cleopatra*), MM is overwhelmed by the many betrayals and honey-traps of those she considers 'friends' that she collapses into a complete emotional meltdown. The non-stop flow of drugs that her 'friend' Peter (Lawford) keeps supplying to MM together "with the after-effects of the abortion" become too much for her.

She was a 'good sport' for both Kennedy brothers: To abort the pregnancies, which they arguably caused, once they "got what they wanted," as MM puts it (MLT, p.264). But MM cannot shake the shameful realization that was but 'a sex object' to them, nothing more than "the butt of filthy corporate jokes" (MLT, p.18). Her future appears bleak at the moment: There appears to be no light at the end of the long dark tunnel. Marilyn has hit rock bottom.

All MM likely wants is to be rubbed out, to escape from all these sudden pressures she faces on virtually all fronts. Retiring to Building #3 (to be alone), MM keeps popping the pills amply supplied by Peter (her erstwhile buddy from Sinatra's Rat Pack).

When Frankie finally returns to see what became of his 'special guest,' he is disgusted and appalled. He asks to see the (Polaroid) photos: He realizes that Marilyn has been compromised: that she is certainly not having a good time, to put it mildly. He requests the photographers to burn all those photos (MLT, p.286-287). And then, when he finally musters the courage to go see Marilyn (alone in building #3), he finds her in a near drug overdose. Rushing her to Emergency to save her life, he must have been reminded of the several times he himself attempted suicide (the first two over Ava Gardner), and how he likewise cheated death by the skin of his teeth.

Joe DiMaggio (who was at Lake Tahoe that same weekend since late Friday night, staying at the Silver Crest Motor Hotel nearby) appears on Sunday (29th July 1962) to have a private chat along the water's edge with MM away from everyone else (MLT, p.285). Although no one knows what was said between these two lovers, it becomes apparent what the end-result is: as Joe, MM's ex-hubby, formally proposes re-marriage on the 1st of August, just three days later.

MM flies back to LA with Pat and Peter Lawford in a private jet. But en route (in a limousine) from the LA International Airport, Peter Lawford leaves the limo to chat with Bobby Kennedy (for more than half-an-hour to warn him "Marilyn had begun making threats"). (MLT, pp 286-287)

12.   31 July 1962: Fox Rehires MM

On Tuesday, 31 July 1962, Darryl F. Zanuck (the new head of Fox) contacted MM to reassure her that she would be officially reinstated with Fox (MLT, pp.270,295-296). Furthermore, Zanuck promised her that he would increase her salary from $100,000 to $500,000 if she would return to work for the 4th of September. MM was ecstatic, to say the least! [MLT, 292,296,347)

13.   03 August 1962: MM and RFK

On this last weekend of MM's life, she appeared to be in a super good mood (according to witnesses, in particular her 'housemaid' Eunice Murray).

She expects an expensive sofa to be delivered to her place this weekend as she had "ordered truckloads of furniture from Mexico" (where it was being 'manufactured') (MLT, p. 61).

> Whatever her source, Monroe knew by midmorning that Bobby [Kennedy], Ethel, and their children were on a jet headed for San Francisco. It was a combined business and vacation trip" (MLT, 298). ["Kennedy and his family spent most of the three-day weekend at the Bates Ranch in Gilroy, California. The Bar Association provided a suite at the St. Francis Hotel for use as an office and retreat during its convention (MLT, p. 298n.).]

Life magazine was promoting MM's nude swimming scene at airport gift shops and newsstands everywhere. This exposé likely reinforced in RFK's mind that any hint of a liaison with MM (especially at that time) could prove damaging to his career, not to mention JFK's. (MLT, p. 299)

To make matters even worse, by early afternoon, as MM keeps her pre-scheduled appointments both with her internist, Hyman Engleberg, and her psychoanalyst Ralph

Greenson, she stops at least three times to call RFK at his St. Francis suite. But RFK refuses to return her calls.

Perhaps by appointment, MM stops in at Frank's Home Nurseries (a tree farm) to select "several citrus trees, flowering plants and succulents" for her new landscaping plans with delivery arranged for the following day. "Very likely she planned her wedding [to Joe Dimaggio (on Wednesday, August 8th)] to be set outdoors, and the garden and pool area needed plantings and colour." (Donald Spoto, *Marilyn Monroe: The Biography*, 1993: pp. 549, 565)

She continues to call Bobby repeatedly but without success.

MM calls Robert Slatzer (who had requested her return call a day earlier before she would take 'action' against the Kennedy brothers) to state emphatically that she wants "Bobby to end 'it' [the dangling unfinished 'Goodbye'!] himself". RFK (it appears) had made many promises to marry MM, to lead her on, to continue their most intimate affair, an affair that involved not mere sex, but apparently MM's feelings, mind, heart, and soul. (MLT, pp. 238,240,251-254,258-259)

MM initially believed Bobby's words, and was sold hook, line, and sinker that he would marry her. Now MM knows that to be a lie, something she wants Bobby to say to her face: That he was a liar and that he lied to her, something she already knows but wants to hear him say 'it'! (MLT, pp. 280,288)

She does not at all appreciate Bobby's crass 'tragic brushoff' and will not settle for less than a full in person apology (especially as he left her alone to deal with aborting 'his' baby, as researchers currently maintain. (MLT, pp. 282-284, 288, 290, 299-300, 407)

To Robert Slatzer, MM renews her threats (to go public) against the Kennedy brothers:

> If I don't hear from Bobby Kennedy before the end of the weekend, I'm going to call a press conference, and blow the lid off this whole damn thing!... I'm going to tell about my relationship with both Kennedy brothers... that the Kennedys got what they wanted out of me, and then moved on! (MLT, p. 299).

MM begins to leak out her disgust and dismay with the way the Kennedys treated her to her confidante, Jeanne Carmen, as well as to Jean Louis's head fitter, Elizabeth Courtney, and others (MLT, p. 299). She demands to meet with her (paid) publicists Rupert Allan and Pat Newcomb, but only Newcomb initially responds. "She felt like a spurned woman and that she had been deliberately used." (MLT, p. 300)

MM speaks with a photographer, George Barris (who was in NYC) to come to see her (at her home in LA) on the weekend (because she has something very important to discuss with him); but he postpones the visit until Monday (6th August, two days after MM's unexpected death). Rupert

Allan finally agrees to meet with MM after the weekend, as well, on 6th August 1962, Monday (MLT, p. 328).

Bobby no doubt (worried about MM's flurry of phone calls) decides to arrange a "wine-and-candlelight approach to ease Monroe out of the picture" (MLT, p. 301). He requests Peter Lawford and Pat Newcomb (who actually works closely with RFK, although on MM's payroll) to arrange a meeting with MM at their favorite cozy Italian restaurant in LA, La Scala. MM agrees.

According to employees at La Scala (MLT, pp. 253-254), as Pat and Marilyn meet Bobby and Peter things shortly escalate to a heated exchange at a back table (MLT, pp. 300-301).

MM and Pat Newcomb retreat to MM's Brentwood home where Pat spends the night in the Guest Room. MM is beside herself and simply cannot sleep. She is interrupted by mysterious phone calls beginning at 11:00 P.M.:

> A female voice screamed at her, 'Leave Bobby alone, you tramp!' Then the woman hung up. A second call came at 12:45 A.M. It was the same woman. 'You'll be sorry if you ever see Bobby Kennedy again!' The calls continued intermittently until 5:30 A.M. (MLT, p. 307).

[Author's Note: As certain parties may speculate, "How is it possible for RFK to meet with MM that Friday night given that he was already at the St. Francis Hotel in San

Francisco earlier that day?", I would relay the explanation given by some as follows:

> The Attorney General, having received Monroe's increasingly strident messages at the St. Francis Hotel..., may have flown down to Hollywood to make a quick nonaggression pact with her. Since he was in San Francisco very early the next morning, he must have flown back to Northern California immediately after dinner. By jet, San Francisco was only a forty-five-minute flight from Los Angeles. (MLT, p. 301)]

14.   04 August 1962: MM Dies

08:30 A.M.

Bright and early on this rather hot August morning, at 8:30 a.m., Norman Jefferies (Eunice Murray's nephew) begins to bring in all his work materials to lay tile in Marilyn's kitchen.

09:00 A.M.

Marilyn awakes to see what he was doing and has a light breakfast.

Patricia (Newcomb) lies peacefully asleep in her bed until she is fully rested (until about Noon), whereas MM has had a fitful night with little to no sleep at all.

Marilyn awaits delivery of a new sofa (from Mexico) [which, as a side note, remains in the shipping crate in MM's home until it is resold (along with Marilyn's other 'effects' from the house) at Christie's Auction in 1999].

11:00 A.M.

Peter Lawford calls MM from the Fox lot to tell MM that RFK's chopper is scheduled to land just after 11:00 a.m. and that they would like to visit MM in her home in Brentwood later this afternoon.

(MLT, pp. 303-306)

MM takes this moment (before RFK's arrival) to once again check out her earlier selection of trees and shrubs at Frank's Home Nurseries (possibly to arrange payment and delivery date?).

12:00 Noon

MM returns around Noon to her home just as Pat (Patricia Newcomb) is awakening. There is a hot discussion between the two of them (according to Norman Jefferies) pertaining to Bobby Kennedy's supposed arrival (which possibly is no surprise to Pat). Marilyn seems to suspect that Pat is currently having an affair with Bobby. Marilyn then tells Pat that her services are no longer required.

01:00 P.M.

Marilyn says that her (psychiatric) 'Nurse' Eunice Murray could also leave (as she typically did leave weekends to go to her own apartment). MM writes a check for severance pay to Mrs. Murray (for $206, which was a lot of money back then); and said that her services were no longer required either.

[Greg Schreiner bought MM's last canceled check (written on 4th August 1962 for $206 USD to Mrs. Eunice Murray) for $100 USD at Christie's Auction in 1999; as well as her still-unpacked sofa which remained in the original shipping crate with the delivery tag date of 4th August 1962.]

Mrs. Murray, however, takes matters into her own hands and immediately calls Dr. Ralph Greenson (who hired Mrs. Murray and who lived less than 2 miles away) to say that Marilyn requires his services.

01:30 P.M.

Dr. Greenson shows up shortly thereafter and states bluntly that Marilyn requires an immediate therapy session with him. Marilyn then accuses Mrs. Murray of being a spy for Dr. Greenson; and sees (for the first time what she often suspected) that they both work together spying on her privacy.

Then MM adds that Dr. Hymen Engelbeg (her regular physician, who also lives close by) was likely in cahoots with Greenson and Murray against her. She also expresses the desire to dismiss him, as well, saying that she was well, and so no longer requires their services.

MM plays a tape recording she made two weeks earlier (as part of her therapy routine) to share with Dr. Greenson that she now feels free of the necessity of all of these $1400/month sessions, that she is free of her romantic ties with the Kennedy brothers (except that she did not like the way they 'dropped her' like a hot potato).

She states that she really did not know how to break it to Bobby that she is no longer interested in him as she has decided to accept Joe DiMaggio's proposal of re-marriage! In fact, she is scheduled to 'fit the dress' she ordered on 6th August, Monday! (MLT, p. 300)

Marilyn had written earlier that she believed "a wise girl leaves [a relationship] before she is left"! Marilyn had wanted to be the one to break up her relationship with Bobby, not the other way around.

She appreciates what Drs. Greenson and Engelberg had done for her but states emphatically that she no longer requires their services. She also states a few very intimate details (we are left to presume) that regard her relationship with Dr. Greenson (which relationship Dr. Engelberg declares later was not professional, nor normal given MM's dependency on him).

This tape as well as all the other taped sessions, MM had with Dr. Greenson were confiscated by the Probate Officer (as Dr. Greenson's "property") and were donated to UCLA to be released to the public at large on 1st January 2039.

What possible good reason could necessitate this very long delay (for 8 decades!) has led many to speculate that Dr. Greenson likely has something to hide, to say the least, in his relationship with MM. He did play (in 1962) the last tape with Mr. John Miner (under a pledge not to reveal the 'intimate contents' portion). However, in 2005, John Miner publishes his extensive notes from these tape recordings in the *L.A. Times* (although not disclosing all the intimate details we may infer).

Miner (as a former L.A. District Attorney) was convinced beyond any reasonable doubt that MM was murdered.

As could be expected, with Miner's death on 25 February 2010, everything he said is currently being discounted by the 'Peter Lawford and Arthur Jacobs Big Lie' theorists who refuse to give up the Big Lie that MM killed MM. (MLT, pp. 286, 312-315, 325-327, 377)

[Author's Sidenote: With both Greenson and Miner deceased at this time, the question remains: Why should we the public have to wait until 2039 to listen to something that should affect neither man? Both men (later) insisted that MM did not commit suicide either accidental or otherwise. (MLT, p. 347)

The conclusion, therefore, is that she was murdered! So why is this vital information still retained from public knowledge? There is no moratorium on murder: MM's case for murder should be opened up so that the Grand Jury could indict these tapes along with all other evidence (from CIA and the FBI files) to investigate the painfully obvious fact: (that) MM was murdered; and, to come to the legal conclusion as to whom the killers were, and the motives of all parties involved.

But Dr. Greenson (who apparently had sex with Marilyn, his patient, as disclosed by Marilyn's close friend, Jeanne Carmen, with whom Marilyn confided in all her secrets) felt that MM could be a threat to not only himself but to the Kennedys should she be allowed to speak to the media Monday morning (06th August 1962) as she had threatened to do so (as disclosed by Mrs. Murray to Greenson).]

MM receives calls at this time from Ralph Roberts (her masseur), Jeanne Carmen, Joe DiMaggio Jr., and even Arthur Miller's dad but they are all answered by Eunice Murray (MM's 'maid') and/or Dr. Greenson himself: MM answers these calls later this evening. ["If someone wants to seriously commit suicide, as Peter Lawford maintains MM did, why should she bother to answer any of these calls?", one may reasonably infer.]

03:00 P.M.

Greenson meets with MM until 3 p.m. at which time he prepares to leave but then instructs Pat (Patricia Newcomb) to leave the premises (as Marilyn had told Dr. Greenson that Pat refused to leave when asked to do so). Pat (who was sunning herself at the back of Marilyn's pool) leaves as requested.

Dr. Greenson instructs Mrs. Murray to stay with Marilyn 'to protect her' this night! [Strange words one would think considering what would happen next.] Mrs. Murray happily agrees to do so (but does not return her severance-pay cheque for $206 that MM wrote for her earlier). Norman

Jefferies remains as well until 7:30 Sunday morning, 5th August 1962.

As Greenson had given Marilyn a sedative (which made her temporarily drowsy and somewhat unsteady), Mrs. Murray had to drive Marilyn to Santa Monica beach to meet with movie director, Elia Kazan (according to one commentator). Kazan and MM meet for an informal discussion. Kazan had directed Marlon Brando in *On the Waterfront* (1954) and earlier in *Streetcar Named Desire* (1951).

As Brando had romantic interests in MM for many years, even sending her flowers and birthday greetings for her 36th birthday (MLT, pp. 39, 87-88, 163, 175, 179), and as MM's contract with Fox would expire soon, it should be no surprise that MM was looking ahead for different and better movie contracts.

Kazan had confessed to a previous love affair with MM in a private letter to his wife, Molly Day Thacher, dated 29th November 1955 (released to *The Hollywood Reporter* in April 2014). It is possible that Kazan felt sympathy to MM's mistreatment by Fox and offered her alternate options.

MM returns home to be meet with RFK and Peter Lawford.

04:15 P.M.

Bobby Kennedy and Peter Lawford are both awaiting MM when she arrives home with Mrs. Murray (according to Norm Jefferies' 1993 testimony; Recorded as: "Norman Jeffries Testimony" in www.angelfire.com). Bernard

Spindell (a former Military Signals Corps technician) had a pirated copy of MM's last day on earth, attests likewise. [He had planted wiretapping devices in MM's home under orders from Jimmy Hoffa (who apparently had a bone to pick with RFK) back in March that year.]

Spindell was later arrested on 15 December 1966. His pirated tape recordings were confiscated from his home by the FBI under Hoover's orders. Although Spindell repeatedly requested the return of those tapes, the FBI has kept them until this day (we are to presume, as they were never returned to Spindell).

According to Spindell's account (from the actual tape recordings of the day's events), Bobby Kennedy was initially soft and polite with MM when they first met in the guest area. But when he asks for 'it' [the listeners presumed he was referring to the 'Red Address/Diary' book in which MM kept a few notes to herself of discussions she had with the Kennedy brothers], MM replies emphatically she does not have 'it'. (MLT, p. 308)

Bobby blows a gasket and raises his voice demanding to have that Address book ASAP. He then marches into MM's private bedroom and begins to ransack (the little that was there) in search of this book, which he claims could mean MM's life if he cannot locate it! MM becomes hysterical (it is claimed) and demands that both men leave her house.

Bobby ignores her demands and keeps opening up drawers and wall panels: He comes across the mesh of wiring hidden by the secret service (and others) behind one of the panels in the closet area. He then realizes that everything he said was likely already recorded and that his visit with MM was a setup.

His first reaction is to blame MM for setting him up for a political fall (along with JFK). MM denies she knows anything about this wiretapping to which Bobby gives her a direct life-and-death threat! He knocks MM against an object which leaves a large bruise on her left hip [which bruise is noted in the later autopsy report]. MM becomes totally unhinged at Bobby's crude manhandling and has an emotional meltdown [MLT, pp. 373-374).

At which point, Peter Lawford intervenes and says to Bobby: "That's enough, Bobby! She really doesn't know anything!" As Bobby leaves, he asks Mrs. Murray to send for Dr. Greenson because MM obviously needs something to calm her down. Mrs. Murray dutifully complies.

04:35 P.M.

Bobby and Peter then left MM to her musings over this whole affair. MM discloses to both Mrs. Murray and Norm Jefferies that Bobby Kennedy had given her a direct 'threat' and that she now feared for her life. Dr. Greenson arrives and gives MM a sedative. He remains with her until 7:00 P.M. shut inside her bedroom.

What they may have discussed or done together in the privacy of MM's bedroom has not been disclosed. But quite likely if the tapes recorded by the various parties that day have still survived, they would likely release what

Spindell (and others who listened to MM's murder that day) have earlier hinted at: That Dr. Greenson became privy to the danger to MM's life that afternoon.

Note of Explanation:

Now it became apparent to all parties listening in at the events that occurred earlier this day at MM's house, that Bobby Kennedy visited MM in her Brentwood home in Hollywood. The trap was set and now it was sprung: Sam Giancana's pressure on the impressionable MM the earlier weekend had borne fruit. Unwittingly MM had demanded Bobby to see her, and unwittingly Bobby complied.

As Sam Giancana already had a CIA contract (through CIA rogue President Sheffield Edwards as admitted and relayed to J. Edgar Hoover) to take out MM only when RFK should arrive at her home, the murder plot swung into full action. Sam (Momo) Giancana was staying at Palm Springs (nearby) awaiting confirmation of MM's death.

[His sickening mindset was typical of psychopaths (as he was thus diagnosed by the military psychiatrists when he went to sign up under the WWII draft: A classic casebook study of a psychopath, they concluded). As the famed psychiatrist, Karl Menninger put it: "In kind, if not in degree, [the psychopaths] then line up with the Marquis de Sade, who believed in pleasure, especially pleasure derived from making someone else feel displeasure." (*Crime of Punishment*, p. 201)]

In a sense, Momo believed that his killing of MM (to blame it on RFK) would be the 'doublecross of the doublecross'. It would be sweet revenge for what RFK and his brother JFK had done to him (and others) in the Bay of Pigs fiasco (17 April 1961) also known as Operation Mongoose.

Since WWII, the secret service (through the US military) had worked with criminals in Italy (as Operation Gladio). The motto of the CIA back then was: 'The enemy of my enemy is my friend' meaning that they would or could work together with the Mafia (in particular with Sam Giancana) to take down Fidel Castro, their mutual 'enemy'. "Momo" was banking on 'making a killing' in Cuba through Casinos run by the Mafia and controlled by himself. The Bay of Pigs disaster (whereby JFK reneged on USA Air Support) ended those 'get rich quick' schemes permanently.

Former US President Dwight D. Eisenhower had passed on this legacy (to take out Castro) to JFK in March 1960, a legacy JFK (and especially RFK) detested. But when the Mafia (and especially Johnny Rosselli, former military sharpshooter, and sniper marksman, had convinced about twelve hundred mercenaries to attempt to take out Castro (believing that the US Airforce would back them up), virtually the entire group was captured except for about one hundred who were killed.

Rosselli somehow escapes and lives to get his revenge on JFK on 22nd November 1963. But unbeknown to "Handsome Johnny" Rosselli, his crime boss, Momo, had accepted the CIA contract to take out MM as soon as RFK would visit her in her Brentwood home.

People have criticized MM for her involvement with the Kennedy brothers saying: "If you are afraid of wolves, stay out of the forest". But then as MM believed she was 'in love,' she truly believed that she was being loved in return (for so is the nature of love: "Love is kind... seeks not her own, is not easily provoked, thinks no evil... bears all things, believes all things, hopes all things, endures all things" (I Corinthians 13:4-7).

At some point, MM realizes that she has to break it to Bobby (Kennedy), that it is over between them. Most likely, this painful realization sinks in (as the therapy tapes to Greenson of 15th July reveal) even before the Kennedys had told her (on 17th July) not to call them anymore.

06:00 P.M.

The third call from Ralph Roberts to MM that day is intercepted by Greenson who bluntly barks out to Roberts that MM is not home. This unpleasant tone of voice to Roberts bothers him, as well as the obvious lie that MM is 'not home': He muses that at least Greenson could have been more polite and said simply: "MM is not available" or that "MM is busy at this time."

07:00 P.M.

Greenson leaves MM but does not give her any pills or additional medication at this time as MM calls her friend Jeanne Carmen (for the second time) to see if she has any sleeping pills but is not able to get through to her. MM begins to return her several calls of the day.

Joe DiMaggio, Jr. calls MM (for the third time) which phone call she answers. They have a pleasant chat about his break-up with his girlfriend, which MM greets with enthusiasm believing it to be a good thing! Later, Joe DiMaggio Jr. testifies that MM was in a superb mood, and rather upbeat.

07:15 P.M.

When the conversation with Joe DiMaggio, Jr. ends, Marilyn in her excitement calls Greenson (who lives only two miles away and), who is preparing for a dinner with (movie star) Eddie Albert and his wife Margo for 8:00 P.M. Greenson notes that Marilyn is in excellent spirits and shares her enthusiasm for Joe DiMaggio, Jr.'s breakup. He reminds Marilyn that should she need him, she should ask Mrs. Murray for Eddie Albert's number.

07:30 P.M.

Peter Lawford calls Marillyn (to apologize for the earlier treatment she went through with Bobby Kennedy and) to invite her for dinner with Pat (Newcomb) and himself. She declines and tells Lawford (according to Lawford's later testimony) to say: "Goodbye!" to Jack, Bobby, and himself as she is 'through with love' and all that nonsense she endured. It is clear for a long time now that MM distrusted Peter Lawford. To put it bluntly, she "hated him" as he was "awfully mean" to her. "Her only relationship was with Pat Kennedy Lawford, Peter's wife" (MLT, pp. 317-318).

Later, Peter thinks that it is an odd message and comments that her speech sounded tired and slurred (which both Greenson and Joe DiMaggio Jr. dispute later saying that MM spoke clearly and distinctly). What is interesting to note, however, is that several people said that it was Peter who was thoroughly inebriated that night, and not Marilyn at all.

08:15 P.M.

MM is going to retire early for the night and bids Mrs. Murray a "Goodnight!" but still keeps her phone by her bedside (according to Mrs. Murray). Normally, when MM is ready to sleep, she leaves the phone in another room and covers it with pillows to muffle its loud ringing sound. She apparently can't sleep despite the earlier sedative Dr. Greenson gave her but continues to phone her phone buddies and to return calls.

08:30 P.M.

Peter Lawford, still puzzled by MM's "Goodbye!" comment to Bobby and himself, calls his brother-in-law, Mickey Rudin (MM's attorney), to ask if he could call Mrs. Murray to see if MM is all right (as he had just called her an hour ago and felt something was amiss). Rudin calls Mrs. Murray to ask if MM is okay, and to check on her, but Mrs. Murray insists that all is well, and that MM had just gone to bed early tonight.

09:30 P.M.

Still excited by the events of the day no doubt, MM finds that she simply cannot drift off to sleep, and as she has no additional medication or pills available, phones her dear friend Jeanne Carmen and does manage to catch her on the phone (on this, the third attempt). She asks Jeanne if she has any extra sleeping pills as MM is completely out of them, but Jeanne tells MM she too has no pills (as the two friends typically shared Nembutal tablets). Marilyn likely tells Jeanne of Bobby's visit and what transpired earlier today. (MLT, 342-343)

10:10 P.M.

As Marilyn tries to sleep, she receives a call from Bill Bonocanno which she quickly interrupts to tell him that she heard some sort of commotion in the house. Marilyn leaves the phone off the hook and goes to investigate the noise. She never returns to the phone.

When MM comes to the Guest room (where she thought the noise came from) she is met with two strangers, Leonard 'Needles' Gianola and James 'Mugsy' Tortorella, two Chicago hitmen sent by Sam Giancana to murder her. The hired thugs act quickly.

They disrobe MM, pin her face down [bruise marks are noted on both her shoulders and lower back during the autopsy], tape her mouth shut, and place the CIA specially designed poison capsule (intended originally for Fidel Castro) as a suppository into MM's rectum. They tape it shut and allow its fast-acting lethal poison to enter into her bloodstream. Within minutes, MM is comatose and non-responsive. They remove the tape and leave.

Meanwhile, both Mrs. Murray and her nephew Norman Jefferies have been detained by two other plain-clothes men: They do not identify themselves but threaten both Eunice and Norman with their very lives should they attempt to call the Police or to intervene in any way. Norman later testifies (in 1993) that he believed they were either CIA or FBI agents because of their dress and demeanor.

10:25 P.M.

Once the men leave, Eunice and Norman enter into the Guest room where MM's body lay motionless; and sense that she is dying. Mrs. Murray immediately calls Peter Lawford and tells him what just transpired. He arrives in minutes with Bobby Kennedy and Patricia Newcomb. Pat Newcomb has a hysterical meltdown upon seeing MM apparently dead, saying out loud: "Marilyn is dead! Marilyn is dead!". Both Bobby and Peter try to calm her down and ask Mrs. Murray to call an Ambulance.

10:35 P.M.

While Natalie Trundy (Jacobs) is attending a Henry Mancini concert at the Hollywood Superbowl for her 21st birthday with her (future) husband, Arthur P. Jacobs (MM's publicist for Fox), they receive a phone call message (from Arthur's employee, Margot Patricia Newcomb) to say that MM is dead. [Arthur Jacobs later disappears for two days without contacting Natalie as to his whereabouts]. He arrives at MM's place before 11:00 P.M.

The Schaeffer Ambulance arrives promptly with James Hall (as the Ambulance driver) and Murray Leibowitz, the attendant. Dr. Greenson is also summoned (probably by Mrs. Murray). After several attempts at CPR with MM, and applying mouth-to-mouth respiration, MM appears to subconsciously react, and color returns to her cheeks.

The Ambulance Driver relates what happens next: A doctor with a black bag arrives (Greenson, it is later confirmed). He states that he is MM's doctor. He takes out a long (heart) syringe from his bag, fills it with a brown fluid, and immediately injects it into MM's heart, moving her naked breast aside with one hand. The syringe is misdirected, hits a rib, but Greenson does not pull it out for a re-try: instead, he forces it down into MM's heart cracking a rib in the process (the distinct rib-cracking sound is heard by the Ambulance driver). He then releases the contents of the large syringe into MM's heart and tells the party present that they must now rush her to the Hospital.

11:10 P.M.

The party present hastily carry MM's nude body into the Ambulance and rush off to the Santa Monica Hospital nearby, leaving Pat Newcomb behind possibly to make a few phone calls, and to chat with her boss, Arthur Jacobs (whom she had likely called earlier at 10:30 P.M.; MLT, p. 310). During the trip, someone notes that Bobby Kennedy says a prayer for MM's recovery.

Before they arrive at the Santa Monica Hospital, Dr. Greenson realizes that MM is gone. The 'candle blowing in the wind' [Elton John] has been snuffed out. Marilyn is no more. RFK, Peter (Lawford), and Dr. Greenson now realize that the jig is up (that MM's death has been orchestrated by devious powers to obviously blacken Bobby's reputation and as a ploy against his brother JFK's bid for re-election).

The decision is made not to continue en route to the hospital but to do damage control ASAP. They return to the scene of the crime (MM's Brentwood home) shortly before midnight (to have MM's body placed back into the Guest suite, as before).

11:45 P.M.

The next-door neighbor, Arthur (Abe) Landau (a LA financier), returns from a party and notes that there is an Ambulance present.

After the Ambulance leaves, Bobby contacts LAPD Police Chief, William Parker, a personal friend of his (and one to whom he had hinted he might make Director of the FBI, as RFK did not like J. Edgar Hoover). Chief Parker agrees to send over his best hand-picked officers for the cover-up.

Bobby Kennedy asks Peter Lawford and Dr. Greenson to accompany him in Peter's dark grey Lincoln Continental sedan as he needs to check out of his L.A. Beverly Hilton Hotel before he takes the helicopter (parked at Fox , MLT, pp. 303-305) to the L.A. Airport, to catch the 2 A.M. flight from L.A. to San Francisco (where RFK will later claim he was present during this entire weekend).

15.   05 August 1962: The Cover-Up

12:10 Midnight

En route to the Beverly Hilton Hotel, Peter Lawford drives (without headlights on) between 70 to 80 miles per hour going East on Olympic Boulevard In L.A. and is stopped and told to pull over at the Robertson intersection by a Hollywood LAPD traffic cop, Officer Lynn Franklin.

Officer Franklin immediately recognizes Peter Lawford and shining his bright flashlight into the back seat, he acknowledges Bobby Kennedy as 'Sir'! But he does not know the passenger in the front seat who is addressed simply as a 'doctor' (until he later sees his photo in the newspaper depicting MM's death).

Although he notes that Peter is inebriated and has the shakes (he keeps trembling as if cold despite the hot summer night), he does not issue them a speeding ticket but instead gives them the correct direction to turn around to arrive at the Beverly Hilton Hotel. He reminds them not to speed and acknowledges (in response to Bobby's question) that they are free to go.

Bobby checks out of the Beverly Hilton Hotel. They then drive Bobby to his 'dark' (tinted) helicopter parked at the

Fox Studio lot. Bobby takes off (where a Secret Service agent is waiting for him) to the L.A. Airport.

Lawford and Greenson return to MM's place.

[Sometime later, the Police Officer Franklin puts two and two together, realizing that the location where he pulled Lawford's car over was only a short distance from MM's place; and discovers that Greenson was MM's psychoanalyst. Franklin notes as well the time of MM's death: The same night that he caught Lawford speeding away from the direction of MM's home.

[As a result of these 'coincidences,' Franklin seriously contemplates (in a later media interview) whether Greenson and RFK had something to do with MM's sudden death. He concludes that it likely was murder.]

12:15 A.M. [Meanwhile at MM's home]

Within minutes, several Police cars arrive, and the LAPD Intelligence Department (part of a 57-member team that specializes in 'Intelligence work' or coverups for the Police Chief) goes to work. According to an eyewitness, Norman Jefferies, the LAPD Intelligence Agents carry MM's (nude) body from the Guest room to her bedroom, where a suicide attempt is staged.

Mrs. Murray is told to wash all the linen sheets and to help clean up MM's soiled body (possibly together with Pat Newcomb?) so that no foul play can be suspected. As a result of the suppository being forced into the rectum of the still struggling MM, there were likely remnants of feces, urine, and blood samples present or excreted.

The Intelligence Officers wipe down all fingerprints of the crime scene (even MM's own prints) in both rooms. Neatly placed empty pill bottles (none of which were prescribed by either Drs. Greenson, or Engelberg) are placed with their caps tightly sealed all in a row next to MM's bed.

She is placed face down (initially) with a phone receiver in her right hand (as seen in one photo). MM is staged as if in a provocative photoshoot position (with a white bedsheet partly covering her nude backside). In their haste, the Agents forget to place an empty glass next to the pill bottles. They make MM's bedroom look completely clean of any evidence of wrongdoing.

[But (as later investigators were wont to say) it looks 'too clean, too perfect, too staged'!]

12:30 A.M.

The Intelligence Officers are left to do their duty, to make the murder of MM appear as a suicide.

Meanwhile, Johnny Rosselli having gained word that MM was indeed murdered (although he initially believed it was done by the Kennedys), goes to Jeanne Carmen's home to tell her that MM has been murdered; and to warn her that her life is therefore in danger (as MM had shared many secrets with her).

As Rosselli had first introduced Jeanne (as he did Marilyn) to his boss Momo, he feels partly responsible for her safety. He tells Jeanne that she needs to flee right now and that he will help her to relocate in Nevada (with her two children). She instantly packs and rushes off for the next fourteen years to live under a new name far away from Los Angeles, never to contact anyone, nor to return until 1976 (after the death of Sam Giancana on 19 June 1975).

[Although never confirmed by Police records who really killed Momo, Jeanne Carmen discloses in an interview that the 'Silver Fox' "Handsome Johnny" Rosselli told her he did it. The actual killing was somewhat graphic. According to this record, Roselli, who was completely trusted by Momo, had come to Momo's place for breakfast. And in the course of their discussion, Rosselli shot Momo, his boss, one bullet in the back of the head. Then as Momo lay dying on his back in a puddle of blood, Rosselli told him (that): "This is for what you did to Marilyn!"; and shot six bullets directly into his face!]

[Apparently, it's explained in various sources that mobsters are okay when they kill their own, but when someone totally innocent, as for example a child, is deliberately 'taken out' on a contract, then other mobsters have a problem with that. Momo's role in the death of both the Kennedy brothers was acceptable for Rosselli (as Rosselli himself by his own admission was involved in JFK's murder).]

[But for Momo to have MM killed bothered Rosselli to the point that he simply had to end this monster's life, knowing full well that his own life would be over not long thereafter.

(Indeed, Rosselli disappeared on 28 July 1976). For, it appears, you cannot kill your own Mafia boss and live long to tell about it.]

01:00 A.M.

MM's next-door neighbor, Arthur (Abe) Landau, again testifies that he saw several police cars and a lot of other persons running around MM's property shortly after 1:00 A.M. They did not begin to leave until sometime around 2:00 A.M. Greenson remains on the scene but ducks all photos that were taken.

Peter Lawford and a private detective (Fred Otash) go over MM's home with a fine-tooth comb to ensure that there is no evidence of a crime anywhere. MM's closet and bedroom which were messed up by Bobby Kennedy (earlier that day) are put in order. A search is out for MM's 'Red Diary' book but it is not located at this time.

Later, on Monday morning 6th August 1962, Mrs. Murray passes on the Red Diary/Address book (which she was hiding for MM) to the Coroner who arrives to pick up information on Ms. Monroe's last known relatives (so that someone may bear the burden of the funeral expenses, as so far no one stepped up to the plate).

MM's much-sought-after Red Diary is glanced through by Dr. Lionel Grandison (one of several coroners for MM's death) who places it for safe-keeping in the mortuary safe intending to go through it more carefully the following morning (in order to locate the next of kin).

[But by the next morning, Tuesday, 7th August 1962, it disappears from the locked safe never to be returned! Grandison and Deputy Chief Coroner Noguchi by now both conclude that MM's autopsy is being tampered with by higher powers, that the entire procedure has become a farce, that MM's death has been treated as a joke, that a well-orchestrated coverup is the only logical explanation (MLT, pp. 325-329].

02:00 A.M.

The Police are packing up, cleaning up the property, and preparing to leave.

Bobby Kennedy catches his 02:00 A.M. flight to San Francisco, about 320 miles away, and arrives there without a hitch.

Mrs. Murray is still doing laundry all through the night, as she has several loads to wash and to dry.

Pat Newcomb, Peter Lawford, Fred Otash, and possibly 'other guests' (Arthur Jacobs, etc.) leave to their respective homes.

Dr. Greenson and Mrs. Murray (with Norman Jefferies present) plan the details of the staged suicide: MM's bedroom window is apparently broken with a fireplace poker from the inside, as most of the shards of glass are found outside the window and some distance from the window frame. The place where the window is broken however is miscalculated as one arguably cannot easily reach one's arm through the broken window to reach the window latch without cutting oneself!

No one believes that Mrs. Eunice Murray ran to MM's window and "looked through the window and saw Monroe on her bed 'looking strange'" (MLT, p. 326) or that Dr. Greenson actually entered MM's bedroom through her bedroom window, as he attests in this coverup story. It's just not feasible. Eunice Murray and Ralph Greenson were lying to the Police (and they knew it!) when they said that 'nothing was out of the ordinary'.

"Everything was out of the ordinary. Monroe never went to sleep in the nude, with the lights on and the curtains open... The thick blackout curtains [in her bedroom] were tacked shut each evening." [These were a special drapery that "fitted over the windows and were attached to the walls with tacks in order to plunge the bedroom into blackness even at noon."]

"Then Monroe would slip on a fresh brassiere... to keep her breasts from sagging." "Monroe did none of these things on her last night. Her having fallen asleep nude in a room ablaze with light should have alerted Murray to foul play unless, of course, Murray was fully aware of what happened." (MLT, pp. 276, 348)

Notwithstanding these glaring inconsistencies, Dr. Greenson's statement on the record is considered gospel truth: It becomes the accepted course of events. (MLT, pp. 326-327)

As to MM's door being locked, the only key to the house was a skeleton key that Mrs. Murray used to lock the front and rear doors late at night. (Mrs. Murray's copy which she always kept with herself is the only key ever found.) As was later noted, none of the doors within the house had keys as the previous owner never gave them to Marilyn, because they were too old and did not work properly anyway.

[According to later testimony (in 1985), Mrs. Murray stated that MM never locked her bedroom door (which did have a deadbolt lock) because of the fear she had ever since her highly traumatic experience on 1st February 1961 when she unwisely admitted herself into the Payne-Whitney Psychiatric Clinic (after the death of her idol, Clark Gable) having blamed herself for his unexpected heart attack on 16th November 1960).

MM, who followed (perhaps unwisely) the advice of her (former) NYC psychiatrist, Dr. Marianne Kris, to enter this Clinic complained later that they "barred the windows and [had] glass panes in the door so that nurses could glance inside" while treating you "like a nut"! (MLL, p. 228)

[She had been locked into a small confinement for long periods of time as part of her therapy. The Psychiatric Nurses forcibly gave her several baths a day occasionally assisted by several staff members who indiscriminately grabbed various parts of her body to submit her to their version of what 'cleanliness' meant. Her treatment was so invasive and intrusive, that she later had to have her gall bladder removed (in June 1961) as well as experienced intermittent bleeding in her vagina for some time thereafter. (MLL, p. 228)

[Marilyn eventually (after a week of this 'therapy') broke down completely. She called Joe DiMaggio to help her and told him that she was trapped inside a Clinic which refused to release her. She felt so stressed out as if she were to die there. As one account describes it, Joe instantly sensed her pain and became her 'white knight'. He arrived at the Clinic almost immediately to demand that they release 'his wife' this very minute.

[Although the Psychiatric Nurses there realized that Marilyn and Joe were legally divorced, Joe created such a loud and angry scene (threatening to tear apart the Clinic with his bare hands) that they quickly released Marilyn to Joe's custody. In one of her darkest moments, Marilyn had no one else to turn to (to escape that 'house of horrors') but Joe DiMaggio.

[MM later comments that when she initially entered the Clinic, she thought that she was experiencing a mental breakdown (as did her mother), but once inside the Clinic she soon realized that the staff members themselves were the 'insane people,' that they were crazier than the inmates, and that the inmates were genuinely 'crazy' people, much more than she thought she could ever be. As a result of this nightmarish treatment, Marilyn (Mrs. Murray admitted) could never again lock her bedroom door.]

03:00 A.M.

Although Mrs. Murray is still doing laundry so late at night, she is called to review the storyline for MM's staged suicide (as follows): Mrs. Murray apparently found MM locked inside her bedroom and notices through the bedroom window (which by the way has a rather heavy blackout curtain) that her light was still on and sees that she is holding her phone in her right hand.

She calls Dr. Greenson, who comes over, uses a fireside poker to smash the window, enters the bedroom through the broken window, and opens the bedroom door. This was the Big Lie that was to be perpetuated through all mainstream media right to this very day. (MLT, pp.326-327)

No one (initially) appears to notice that there is no empty glass next to MM's several empty bottles of pills. As MM apparently could not swallow even one Aspirin without a large sip of water, how she could swallow the 70 to 90 capsules they (later) claimed she swallowed (based upon the extremely high overdosage found in her liver, at least 3-5 times the lethal dosage) remains a mystery: a gross miscalculation by the 'suicide' theorists!

One would think that if all these capsules were orally ingested, that MM would have long died before she reached the minimum 3-5 times the lethal dosage limit?!

> The most likely argument against suicide or accidental death came from the Suicide Prevention Team. 'Marilyn would have had to gulp down those pills, all of them [70 to 90], within a matter of min-

utes, a very few minutes,' said Robert Litman, the UCLA psychiatrist who headed the Team. 'If she had taken those pills a few at a time, she would have been unconscious before she could ingest the amount needed to achieve that degree of barbiturates in her bloodstream.' (MLT, p. 345)

If for instance it were presumed MM had by some magic feat been able to swallow 70-90 capsules without water, how could her suicide be 'accidental'? It had to then be a deliberate suicide!

But to be deliberate was utterly ridiculous: MM had too many exciting things to live for! She was planning a remarriage to Joe DiMaggio. She was in excellent (albeit a bit fatigued) spirits that night. But most important of all: There was absolutely not the slightest trace of any drugs or remnants of capsules throughout her entire digestive tract: not a speck!

Her liver was overloaded with deadly chemicals that could only have entered through the anus: the lower part of her large intestine next to the rectum being darkly discolored. An enema or suppository was the only means possible, as no needle marks were to be discovered anywhere. But a forced enema was not likely because an involuntary enema would have caused serious internal damage, and no such injury was noted in the autopsy (MLT, pp. 342-247).

[The large syringe that Greenson placed into MM's chest did not leave a trace apparently as MM had been turned face down in her 'death position' for several hours allowing the blood to surface to that area and effectively erase that needle mark, we are told. This phenomenon of erasing possible needle marks is known as lividity; that is, "when the blood in the body drops to the lowest point of gravity the part (of the body) the victim is lying on (as, for example 'face down')"; *Webster's Dictionary.*]

03:15 A.M.

Dr. Greenson decides to call Dr. Hymen Engelberg, MM's personal physician, to confirm MM's death.

03:45 A.M.

Dr. Engelberg (who is not privy to this Big Lie theory and staged suicide) arrives and confirms MM is dead. Dr. Greenson already knows that MM was dead (for several hours), but it is necessary to have Dr. Engelberg come over to make the 'story of MM's suicide' appear more credible.

The word eventually leaks out to several key media centers over the next hour that MM is dead! Then the news begins to spread like wildfire to well over 400 outlets.

04:25 A.M.

Dr. Greenson then calls the LAPD to report a death, that MM is dead.

04:35 A.M.

Sergeant Jack Clemmons, a 15-year-old veteran of the LAPD (who happened to be only minutes away), arrives to investigate Ms. Monroe's death. He is stunned to see that this suicide has clearly been staged. He states in his report that MM did not commit suicide and that her death, if not accidental, was therefore 'murder' by deductive logic. He notices that her body position is not in a convulsive state (typical of drug overdose victims) and that there was no white mustache around the lips, or vomit on the sheets or any excretions whatsoever, which would typically be present for overdose suicide victims.

He also noted that the housemaid was still doing laundry all through the night and that there was no drinking glass for the empty tablet bottles, every bottle cap of which was screwed on tightly and the bottles neatly placed in a row. The window was broken in from the inside (despite the loud rebuttals by Dr. Greenson) as most of the broken glass could be seen outside the window. He could not find any key to lock or unlock Ms. Monroe's door. It apparently could not be locked by a key from the inside.

Sgt. Clemmons also notes that when he called the phone service to see to whom MM had last spoken, he was told that all MM's phone records have already been seized by the FBI, and that they are not available to be seen by anyone. The puzzling query that could not escape Sgt. Clemmons's mind was: How did the FBI know that MM was already dead? Jack Clemmons thought that he was the first Official Police Officer to know of MM's death?! Clemmons concludes that whoever seized the phone records likely knew who killed MM. So noting all of these discrepancies, Sgt. Clemmons files his report.

Sgt. Clemmons wants to declare MM's death as a 'crime scene' but senior (actually, 'hand-picked') officers (Sergeant Robert Bryon and Lieutenant Grover Armstrong, Chief of Detectives in West L.A.) arrive from the LAPD and take over the investigation. They refuse to declare this 'obvious suicide' (as Dr. Greenson claims it to be), as a 'crime scene'.

Sgt. Clemmons overhears one of the investigative team members present saying: "Just another case of a Hollywood junkie overdosing." As they could not see any evidence of a struggle or of violence, all fingerprints having been wiped clean, all evidence (what little was left on the scene) is therefore not saved, nor tagged, nor documented. The Jury, they assume, is in: MM murdered MM.

05:00 A.M.

Patricia Newcomb, MM's (former) publicist, arrives wearing dark sunglasses (which she never removes) to introduce several News Reporters and Fox Studio personnel to the death scene. MM's private home becomes a veritable Grand Central Station, as no attempt is made by the Police or anyone else to control the flood of media photographers from traveling throughout MM's home:

> After the Secret Service, the Los Angeles Police Department, and the publicity department at Twentieth Century-Fox were through at Monroe's house, not a scrap of paper remained. Even the

five drawers of Twentieth Century-Fox contracts had disappeared... Evidence shows that much of the document-burning and political tidying up was a collaboration between [Peter] Lawford and Twentieth Century-Fox. (MLT, pp. 350-351)

Many personal items disappear (MM's panties placed on her bedside lampshade, for example, as originally noted in one of MM's early bedroom photos). As well as any possible evidence of a murder or crime scene, while MM's nude body lies partly draped in her private bedroom. Mrs. Murray attempts to restrict passersby from going throughout the house as if it were a museum but to little avail.

05:30 A.M.

Possibly because it is rather early on a Sunday morning, the Los Angeles County Coroner's Office is still not available to do an autopsy until after 08:30 A.M. As MM's body has been decomposing in the rather hot LA August heat since her death approximately 10:30 P.M. earlier that night, a phone call is made from an 'unknown party' [or a party that wished to remain anonymous.

I suspect by deductive logic the caller was Patricia Newcomb] to Allan Abbott and Ron Hast of the Abbott & Hast Mortuary Accommodation Company to come to the Westwood Village Mortuary (at Westwood Village Park Memorial Cemetery) to meet with the (ambulance-style) station wagon that will transport MM's body to them for an initial inspection.

There is no funeral hearse (or limousine) for MM at this time. She is wheeled out in an ambulance stretcher wrapped in a blue blanket. And then driven to be viewed by the Mortuary staff. However, the paparazzi follow the car to the Westwood Village Mortuary attempting to take more photos of MM. To reduce the near violence of dozens of reporters clamoring to catch a photo of MM through the windows of the Mortuary, her nude body is wheeled into a large maintenance closet.

[It is solely my personal judgment in piecing together this narrative from over fifty disparate sources, that one possible explanation for this temporary relocation of MM's corpse is simply to allow her a little respect (if even in death) from the flood of photographers and news reporters who were literally inundating this small somewhat modest abode in Brentwood, especially entering at random into the privacy of her bedroom where her nude body lay displayed partly clad on her bed face down.

[As Pat Newcomb was truly emotionally overwhelmed at MM's sudden death (and suspecting 'foul play' at work), the least she could do, one would think, is to hide MM's body (as an act of human dignity) from the leering gaze of so many strangers and photographers (whom she swore at, calling them, "Vultures!")].

[Hopefully, when the books are open and the records disclosed in 2039, all controversies will be made abundantly clear. For now, there are (admittedly) a lot of missing pieces of MM's last day on earth. Thankfully, sufficient testimonials have been disclosed until now to yield a somewhat focused (if not perfectly clear) kaleidoscope of the events of that fateful day as they unfolded virtually hour by hour.]

05:45 A.M.

Sergeant Clemmons files his official Police Report on the mysterious death of MM claiming that in his opinion MM did not murder herself but that foul play was at work here. Although submitted, his report is never filed (unbeknown to him). Years later, when he asks to see his previously filed report for a television interview, it cannot be found. It disappeared without a trace, not even a record posted that it was indeed ever filed.

06:04 A.M.

Peter Lawford calls JFK to inform him that MM is dead. They chat for about twenty minutes (according to the White House phone log). No need to call RFK, as he already knows.

07:30 A.M.

Norm Jefferies leaves MM's home at this time (according to his 1993 testimony) as the aftermath of MM's death and subsequent intrusion into her home winds down. Coroner Bob Dambacher and Deputy Coroner Cleet Pace receive a phone call to arrange for the pickup of MM's body which is waiting at The Westwood Mortuary.

08:00 A.M.

MM's nude body is covered with a blue blanket as she is transported from the Westwood Village Park Cemetery Chapel by the Morticians Abbott & Hast to the L.A. Coroner's Office (amid a swarm of photographers who want to take photos of MM's nude corpse. But they are denied access to her autopsy (which autopsy lasts five hours).

08:45 A.M.

Chief Deputy Coroner Thomas Tsunetomi Noguchi begins to examine MM's body together with John Miner, the Legal Medical Official who is also the Assistant Deputy Attorney for L.A. They both use magnifying glasses, and both go over every square inch of MM's nude body examining all her orifices, etc. looking for possible needle marks. They conclude that they could not locate anything suspicious.

Upon slicing up MM and taking out her internal organs (her heart, lungs, liver, kidneys, stomach, intestines, colon, etc.), Dr. Noguchi makes the startling discovery that there are absolutely zero remnants of pills or capsules within MM's entire digestive tract. The only organ to show any sign of a death caused by drug overdose is the liver.

Dr. Noguchi takes samples of all of the organs and of MM's blood, and places MM's organs in a safe place for future evidence to show that MM did not die a suicide, but that clearly foul play was at work.

As there were no needle marks, and no indication of ingestion of pills, the only way she could have received such a very high lethal dosage (estimated at least 3 to 5 times the lethal limit) was through a very deadly enema or suppository. MM's lower colon (next to the rectum) indicated a dark purplish discoloration obviously from an extremely lethal suppository. (MLT, pp. 342-346)

Later, Dr. Noguchi will return to his lab to discover all MM's internal organs and samples to be missing (which could substantially prove she did not die from ingesting pills, as was hastily assumed) except for her liver and blood sample (which indicated a high degree of Nembutal and Chloral Hydrate, the latter drug never having been prescribed by any physician to MM). (MLT, p. 334)

[The six CIA specially designed poison pills that were given to Sam Giancana to use for Fidel Castro (of which at least one was used on MM the night of her murder) contained lethal overdosages of both Nembutal and Chloral Hydrate, estimated at fifteen times the lethal dosage per pill.]

09:30 A.M.

Robert Kennedy attends mass at St. Mary's Roman Catholic Parish with his wife Ethel and their 4 children in Gilroy CA 79 miles south of San Francisco. He claims he was in San Francisco for the entire weekend, that he never visited MM's place since 27th June 1962 (when he was noted to speak to her about ending her relationship with JFK). He is not at all surprised to hear of MM's death, we are told.

02:00 P.M.

After MM's autopsy, her body is then driven back to Westwood Village Mortuary where Abbott & Hast prepare her body for viewing, for the Funeral Services to be held 1 P.M. Wednesday on 8th August 1962 at Westwood Village Park Memorial Chapel.

04:00 P.M.

The Hollywood Columnist, Sidney Skolsky (1905-1983) said: "On the Sunday they found Marilyn dead [05 August 1962], I had an appointment with her for that afternoon at Four to work on *The Jean Harlow Story*." (MLL, p.112)

MM surely did not plan, nor wish to miss this interview: she looked forward to this meeting, it can well be assumed.

C. The Aftermath

1.   06 August 1962: The Day After

MM's red address/diary book (which was finally located and) given by Mrs. Eunice Murray to the Coroner's office Monday morning, 6th August 1962, (to facilitate the knowledge as to her next of kin) goes missing the same night it was discovered and placed in the safe in the mortuary. Again, criminal activity is suspect here: No notes of supervision, no record-keeping, no documentation of MM's death, and the proceedings of her autopsy can be located to this day.

When police detectives finally begin to ask questions to suggest that Monroe might have been murdered, Dr. Noguchi calls for his test results from the Lab. But he is curtly informed by his superiors that the test results have been discarded. "An official memo said that 'further tests are unnecessary as the death has been declared to be a suicide.' Noguchi's carefully preserved tissue samples had been inexplicably discarded on orders of Chief Toxicologist Raymond Abernathy." (MLT, p. 334).

All Deputy Chief Coroner Thomas Noguchi could do to inform the public of these charades is to publish his book *Coroner to the Stars*, (in 1983). He states that he did not believe MM committed suicide based on the evidence he had originally examined, which evidence conveniently disappeared from a safe and secured location, so as to take away the possibility to prove medically that MM was murdered. As a result of these disclosures in his book, Dr. Noguchi is demoted as "Deputy Chief" Coroner in 1983.

In the fall-out from MM's untimely death, a deal is struck between RFK and J. Edgar Hoover. In exchange for the coverup assistance from the FBI, with J. Edgar's promise not to release MM's highly sensitive phone log (records), J. Edgar demands that RFK make his position as Director of the FBI permanent effective immediately.

And given that J. Edgar did not intervene to protect MM from these murderous thugs (although his agents were dutifully recording all the events in a van nearby), J. Edgar wanted RFK to state that due to J. Edgar's great work in stemming the flow of Communism (MM being the most recent victim as an undoubtedly 'communist agent', via her marriage with her former husband Arthur Miller) he, J. Edgar, would be awarded a lifetime position as Director of 'his FBI'.

Early Monday morning, 6th August 1962, RFK did just that. A trade-off was struck: MM's life for J. Edgar's tenured position. With MM's death, business as usual resumed. (MLT, p. 373)

What we can take away from this gross injustice to MM is that "power [especially political power] always has to be kept in check; power exercised in secret, especially under the cloak of national security, is doubly dangerous" (William Proxmire).

Or as C.S. Lewis so aptly described it:

The greatest evil... is conceived and ordered (moved, seconded, carried and minuted) in clean, carpeted, warmed, well-lighted offices, by quiet men with white collars and cut fingernails and smooth-shaven cheeks who do not need to raise their voices!

2.　08 August 1962: MM's Funeral

MM's funeral is held at Westwood Village Memorial Park Cemetery and is completely paid for by Joe DiMaggio who restricts attendees to only close friends of MM, totaling 31 persons. Frank Sinatra, Dean Martin, Peter Lawford, Pat Kennedy Lawford, and other Hollywood celebrities (as well as all the Kennedys) were excluded.

> My favourite tribute to Marilyn will always be her eulogy by her mentor, Lee Strasberg (President and Founder of the New York Actors' Studio) on Wednesday after 1 p.m. on 8th August 1962 at Westwood Village Park Memorial Cemetery:
>
> Marilyn Monroe was a legend! In her own lifetime, she created a myth of what a poor girl from a deprived background could attain. For the entire world, she became a symbol of the eternal Feminine! But I have no words to describe the myth and legend, nor would she want us to do so. I did not know this 'Marilyn,' nor did she. We gather here today, who knew only 'Marilyn', a warm human being, impulsive and shy, and lonely, sensitive, and in fear of rejection, yet ever

avid and polite, and reaching out for fulfilment.

I will not insult the privacy of your memory of her, a privacy she sought and treasured, by trying to describe her whom you know to you who knew her. In our memories of her, she remains alive, not only a shadow on the Screen, or a glamorous personality. For us, Marilyn was a devoted and loyal friend, a colleague constantly reaching for perfection. We shared her pain and difficulties, and some of her joys. She was a member of our family. It's difficult to accept the fact that her zest for life has been ended by this dreadful accident.

Despite the heights and brilliance, she had attained on the Screen, she was planning for the future. She was looking forward to participating in many exciting things which she planned. In her eyes and in mine, her career was just beginning. The dream of her talent which she had nurtured as a child was not a mirage. When she first came to me, I was amazed at the startling sensitivity which she possessed, and which had remained fresh and undimmed struggling to express itself despite the life to which she had been subjected.

Others were as physically beautiful as she was, but there was obviously something more in her, something that people saw and recognized in her performances, and with which they identified. She had a luminous quality: a combination of wistfulness, radiance, and yearning that set her apart, and yet made everyone wish to be part of it, to share in the childish naiveté which was at once so shy and yet so vibrant. This quality was even more evident when she was on the stage.

I'm truly sorry that you and the public that loved her, did not have the opportunity to see her as we did, in many of the roles that foreshadowed what she would have become. Without a doubt, she would have been one of the really great actresses of the stage.

Now it is all at an end. I hope that her death will stir sympathy and understanding for a sensitive artist and woman who brought joy and pleasure to the world.

I cannot say: "Goodbye!". Marilyn never liked [the sound of]: "Goodbye!" And in the peculiar way she had of turning things around so that they faced reality, I will say: 'Au Revoir!'. For the country to which she has gone, we must all someday visit!

Marilyn Monroe Eulogy: Read by Lee Strasberg 1962
https://www.youtube.com/watch?v=Q-qLyOc97G0

Both Joe DiMaggio and his son, Jr., felt that MM's death was not a suicide. They suspected foul play but could prove nothing conclusive at the time. No one (who was present at and privy to MM's death) would volunteer to speak the truth of what actually occurred. (MLT, p. 380)

3.   17 August 1962: Inquest Day

Ironically, on the very day of MM's Inquest (to determine whether she committed suicide or was murdered) the two key witnesses, Mrs. Eunice Murray, and Patricia Newcomb, each received generous amounts of (hush) money, and given plane tickets to leave the USA for Europe (France, Germany, Italy, Switzerland!) for the next six months!

Mrs. Murray after six weeks of traveling across Europe became bored (as she admitted) and returned home to L.A.; whereas, Patricia Newcomb after two months of globe-trotting returned to a rather prominent executive position next to RFK's office. She never again spoke of MM, nor of that last day of MM's life, even though she was officially MM's publicist (a somewhat contradictory role one might think?)!

[Mrs. Murray, however, did break down in 1985 when interviewed by Anthony Summers for his new book, *Goddess: The Many Lives of Marilyn Monroe* (1985), in which she stated (when she thought the recorders were turned off), that MM did not die a suicide, and that RFK did visit her in her home on that last day of her life.]

Both Assistant Coroners, Thomas Noguchi, and Lionel Grandison refused to sign the cause of death in MM's autopsy report "as a suicide". They said that there was insufficient evidence to demonstrate suicide, as well that the disappearance of all key evidence to prove otherwise is highly suspicious of a cover-up.

But the Chief Coroner, Theodore Curphy, promised them that the evidence and proof of suicide were forthcoming, that they should trust his judgment and decision, and that they should sign the cause of death as: "suicide."

The Assistant Coroners both adamantly refused: They said they would sign it as a 'possible suicide' at best. But Curphy argued for a 'probable suicide' judgment, which (with the promise of further proof and documentation forthcoming [which never came]) they reluctantly, and under protest, did finally agree to label MM's death as a 'probable suicide' just before the 23rd August 1963.

4.   20 August 1962: Ralph Greenson

Under pressure from the Inquest Committee and numerous News reporters hounding Dr. Greenson for a more detailed summary, for more information regarding that last day on Marilyn Monroe's life, Dr. Greenson slips this wild remark into one of his interviews: "If you really want to know what happened to MM, why don't you ask Robert Kennedy?". He then refuses to comment further.

Two years after MM's mysterious death (in August 1964), Greenson is asked once again what did he mean by his caustic remark (in 1962) to "ask Robert Kennedy" if we want more answers to MM's death?

Greenson gives the following noteworthy response (which I quote in his own words): "I can't talk about it, because I can't tell the whole story. I can't explain myself or defend myself without revealing things that I don't want to reveal.

You can't draw a line and say: 'Well, I'll tell you this, but I won't tell you that.' It's a terrible position to be in: to have to say, I can't talk about it, because I can't tell the whole story... Listen, you know, talk to Bobby Kennedy!".

Greenson never again spoke publicly about MM's death but became a sort of recluse, saying he tried to save MM but in the end he 'hurt her'?! We are left to draw our own conclusions.

5.   23 August 1962: Coroner's Report

Chief coroner, Theodore Curphy, provided the following 'proof' and summary of the 'probable suicide' of MM, as his 'opinion':

[As will be noted in this 'conclusion or summary report', there is absolutely zero scientific or medical evidence of anything remotely resembling 'proof of suicide'; in fact, the exact opposite is true: This report is based on hearsay and subjective assumptions made of the psychological and mental state of Ms. Monroe, something coroners have no training, nor expertise to even comment on. But such it is, and so it passed as a 'coroner's opinion', as the cause of MM's death:]

> Ms. Monroe had suffered from psychiatric disturbance for a long time. She had often expressed wishes to give up, to withdraw, and even to die. On more than one occasion in the past when disappointed and depressed, she has made a suicide

attempt using sedative drugs. On these occasions, she had called for help and had been rescued. From the information collected about the events of the evening of August the 4th, it is our opinion that the same pattern was repeated except for the rescue. On the basis of all information obtained, it is our opinion that the case is a probable suicide.

D. Marilyn Is Remembered

1.   My Own Conclusion

Susan Strasberg, one of MM's closest friends, described the legacy of MM as that of the lotus that grows in the mud! Ms. Strasberg added: "MM continues to rise [in posthumous fame] no matter how people try to pull her down"! There is a large grain of truth to Susan Strasberg's words: The implication is that there are still people who would like to "pull her down"! I see this verdict, this slur of "probable suicide" as one such instance.

The week following MM's 'suicide' (falsely so claimed), the suicide rate in the USA initially doubled and then tripled for the rest of August! Incredible how negative the effect was on those 'close to the edge', who looked up to MM and therefore who concluded (wrongly) that if MM can simply give up, a woman 'so sunny and so funny', then why should I resist the temptation to also commit suicide?

Such a travesty of Justice. Marilyn Monroe did not murder Marilyn Monroe! To conclude otherwise is The Biggest Lie yet perpetrated on Western Civilization! Consider MM's own words: "There are only three choices in life: Give up, Give in, or Give it all you've got!". These do not sound at all like the words of a basket case, a drug floozy, someone who gives up ending it all!

Consider who would benefit if MM should be labeled as a victim at her own hand:

The #1 Party: JFK and RFK: If MM's death is determined to be a suicide, RFK then could not have murdered her. So, his political power is secured as well as that of his elder brother JFK. But their desire for political fame was to be short-lived, as history points out.

It was all for nothing: To dismiss MM as a junkie, as a joke, as someone who did not deserve to have the truth told about the reality of her death, the true nature and hidden motives behind her untimely death was a grave moral mistake. But one which given time will eventually be set straight.

The #2 Party: Fox Studios: To benefit from a 'probable suicide' judgment Fox had a $13 million Agent Insurance clause on MM. If she was murdered by an outside party, then Fox could not collect that large bounty on her head (because 'that party' would have to pay for those legal costs and 'damages').

Recall that no one (at first) stood up for this orphan girl? No one came to the mortuary to claim her body, no family member, no member of the Strasberg family, or Dr. Greenson, or any of her relatives, all to whom she gave large sums of money and who would inherit her possessions!

Not even Fox offered to cover MM's funeral costs. Imagine that. It has been estimated that in the ten years MM made movies for Fox, they earned over $200,000,000 from her top-notch performances! Yet they never gave her any credit, not as an actor, only as a Box Office Star.

Today, those two hundred million dollars MM earned for Fox are estimated to be worth (in 2021) not less than $2,000,000,000.00 (that's $2 Billion)! For all this money, yet Fox would not cover MM's basic funeral expenses. Only Joe DiMaggio stepped up to the plate and hit another home run. He proved his love for MM and made it public for eternity. He agreed, in the absence of anyone else, to cover all MM's funeral costs.

But if MM's death could be deemed a 'suicide' or at least a 'probable suicide', then Fox Studio could collect from that 'straw head' (as Darryl Zanuck, the head of Fox, liked to call her) the $13 million they needed to help finance their dud of a movie, *Cleopatra*, which originally cost $44 million (but eventually reached $62 million by the end of production)! It appears even to this day that the only value Fox Studio (and other movie moguls) could see in MM was as a 'cash cow'.

But thanks to a flood of testimonials in the past six decades, we have a much different story than that of The Big Lie (that "MM murdered MM"): In order for the evil of big lies to succeed, all that is necessary is for good people to do nothing.

Perhaps the world needs more anger for the disrespect and disgrace heaped upon MM in this major cover-up of her murder? Perhaps the world allows evil to succeed, simply because it isn't angry enough?

As John Steinbeck asks: "Must the hunger [for justice] become anger and the anger fury before anything will be done?". Or as MM puts it in her own words: "Always be yourself. Retain individuality. Listen to the truest part of yourself."

2.   Reflections on MM

At the end of an interview with George Barris (only weeks before her untimely death) MM closed the interview with these cheerful words: "As far as I'm concerned, the happiest time of my life is right now! There's a future and I can't wait to get to it! It should be interesting!" (MHOW, p.138) Hardly the words of a despondent, depressed Marilyn (who wanted to take her own life) as the media propogandist paint this dreary picture, one would think!

Some may consider this 'thought-experiment' to be a work of fiction, a product of an overactive imagination; whereas others, may see this work for what it is: An exposé into probably the biggest whopper ever put across the thinking minds of the world today. Either way, in 2039, when (the masks come off and) all known documents (currently hidden in secret CIA and FBI files) come to light, what an explosive event that should prove.

But until then, allow me to leave this thought that should be chewed over carefully: "If they can kill MM, the most popular (and, arguably, the most well-beloved) female movie star in history, and completely 'get away with it', then they can kill anyone in the world, even the President of the United States, with total impunity."

What a chilling thought! How pervasive this Big Lie has become! How glorious the day when it shall be exposed, and the myth exploded that MM murdered MM!

In honor of MM's memory, allow me to share this concluding thought (as she always did say: "Hold a good thought for me!"):

(From Romeo & Juliet)

"Death lies on her like an untimely frost,
Upon the sweetest flower of all the field"!

[Or as MM said of herself: "I never wanted to be Marilyn: It just happened. Marilyn is like a veil I wear over Norma Jean."]

If I were present the day MM died, I would have liked to have paraphrased the following:

(as originally exclaimed by Gaius Octavius upon hearing of the death of Mark Antony, in *Cleopatra*)

Is that announced as simply as that?

Marilyn is dead?
Marilyn Monroe is dead!

The soup is hot!
The soup is cold!
Marilyn is living!
Marilyn is dead!

Shake with terror when such words pass your lips...

The dying of such a woman
Must be shouted, SCREAMED!

It must be echoed back from
The corners of the Universe!

Marilyn is Dead!
Norma Jeane is dead!
Marilyn Monroe lives no more!

3.   Marilyn Monroe's Charisma

Fox screen writer, Nunnally Johnson, perhaps best summed up the early prevailing attitude towards MM: "She is a phenomenon of nature, like Niagara Falls, or the Grand Canyon. You can't talk to it. It can't talk to you. All you can do is sit back and be awed by it." (MLT, pp. 23-24)

Marilyn was a fighter: she was a survivor! She well knew (as she said in *Gentlemen Prefer Blondes!*): "I can be smart when it's important, but most men don't like it!". Yes, Marilyn accepted her limitations as a 'national institution' (as well-known as 'hot dogs, apple pie, or baseball').

Nonetheless, she knew she belonged to the public and to the world, not because, as she said: "I was talented or even beautiful, but because I had never belonged to anything or anyone else." The public became Marilyn's surrogate mother (in a sense) as she lacked the sympathy and warmth than normally would be granted most children in life.

As Katherine Butler Hathaway puts it so well:

> Everybody knows that a good mother gives her children a feeling of trust and stability. She is their earth. She is the one they can count on for the things that matter most of all... She is the one they want to be near when they cry... There is no substitute for her. Somehow even her clothes feel different to her children's hands from anybody else's clothes. Only to touch her skirt or her sleeve makes a troubled child feel better.

In some magical way of transference, Marilyn was able to receive this sort of moral support from her fans. She often spoke of the upbeat way in which the men (the US Marines) fighting in Korea praised her and accepted her with unabashed adulation when she performed ten shows there in four days (during her honeymoon to Joe DiMaggio). She even kept a photo of that event in her purse to the time of her death. She bonded so well with her audience. And likewise, her audience bonds with her even to this day.

It has been noted that the famed singer Mariah Carey bought Marilyn Monroe's baby Grand piano for $662,500 at Christie's Auction a few years ago (1999). In addition, her famous birthday dress in which she sang "Happy Birthday, Mr. President!" to JFK in May 1962 (and for which she paid $12,000 back then) sold in 1999 at Christie's Auction for $1.4 million.

And then a few years later the same dress at Julien's Auction sold for a whopping $4.81 million, to become the most expensive dress in all history. Even her Raven Black 1956 Ford Thunderbird sold in November 2018 at Julien's Auction for $490,000).

Why all this adulation? Why is it so special to actually want to possess something that Marilyn Monroe once wore or once played or once owned? It makes you wonder: Marilyn was not simply a physical symbol, someone who appealed to men only; she equally appealed to women too.

4.   Accolades for Marilyn Monroe

As Marvin Runyon, the US Postmaster General described Marilyn (on the announcement of US postage stamps made in her honour):

> Being the most famous face in the world would be plenty for a lot of us. The camera loved her and so did we. But she fought to master her craft and earned the respect of the critics in the same way that she won the hearts of millions of fans. Today, more than thirty years after her death, her comedic style still makes us laugh. Her big-girl looks and little-girl voice still makes us smile. And her incredible beauty still stirs our hearts. There is only one: Marilyn!

But my favourite tribute to Marilyn will always be her eulogy by her mentor, Lee Strasberg (President and founder of the New York Actors' Studio) on Wednesday after 1 p.m. on 8th August 1962 at Westwood Village Park Memorial Cemetery (which I quote in part).

> Marilyn Monroe was a legend!... Despite the heights and brilliance, she had attained on the Screen, she was planning for the future. In her eyes and in mine, her career was just beginning... She had a luminous quality: a combination of wistfulness, radiance, and yearning that set her apart, and yet made everyone wish to be part of it, to share in the childish naiveté which was at once so shy and yet so vibrant. This quality was even more evident when she was on the stage.

Following this eulogy, Joe DiMaggio (her second husband who had just formally proposed re-marriage with Marilyn on 1st August 1962, days before her death) kissed Marilyn on the lips saying: "I love you! I love you!" as they permanently closed the lid of her casket.

Years later when Joe was dying (in 1999), his lawyer stated that 'Jolting Joe's' last words were: "I'll finally get to see [my] Marilyn!".

E.   Sources Consulted

1.   Books and Articles

Barham, Patte B. & Brown, Peter Harry. *Marilyn: The Last Take*. Toronto: Dutton, 1992.

Brashler, William. *The Don: The Life and Death of Sam Giancana*. New York: Ballantine, 1977.

Capell, Frank A. *The Strange Death of Marilyn Monroe*. Indianapolis: Herald of Freedom, 1964.

Carroll, Ronald H. (Assistant District Attorney), and Alan B. Tomich (Investigator). "Reinvestigation of the Death of Marilyn Monroe," report of the L.A. County District Attorney's Task Force, December 1982. [See also: FBI File 66-1700-39]

Giancana, Antoinette, and Thomas C. Renner. *Mafia Princess: Growing Up in Sam Giancana's Family*, New York: Morrow, 1984.

Guiles, Fred Lawrence. *Legend: The Life and Death of Marilyn Monroe*. New York: Stein and Day, 1984.

Hoyt, Edwin P. *Marilyn: The Tragic Venus*. London: Robert Hale, 1967.

Hudson, James A. *The Mysterious Death of Marilyn Monroe*. New York: Volitant, 1968.

Mailer, Norman. *Marilyn: A Biography.* New York: Grosset & Dunlap, 1973. [See also, FBI report filed on 23 July 1973 that warned J. Edgar Hoover that Mailer was suggesting "that Bobby Kennedy might have been involved in Monroe's death]

Pepitone, Lena, and William Stadiem. *Marilyn Monroe Confidential.* New York: Pocket Books, 1980.

Sciacca, Tony. *Who Killed Marilyn Monroe?* New York: Manor, 1976. [See also, the Mafia bugging of Monroe's home in FBI File 67-B (1962)]

Slatzer, Robert. The Strange Life and Curious Death of Marilyn Monroe. New York: Pinnacle, 1974.

Spada, James. Peter Lawford: The Man Who Kept the Secrets. New York, Bantam, 1991.

Speriglio, Milo. *Marilyn Monroe: Murder Coverup.* Van Nuys, CA: Seville Publishing, 1982. [See also, L.A. Police Department document number 62-509-403]

Strasberg, Susan. *Bittersweet.* New York: Putnam's, 1980.

Summers, Anthony. *Goddess: The Secret Lives of Marilyn Monroe.* New York: Macmillan, 1985.

Tass Reports (5 in total). KGB Files: "The Kennedys and the Death of Marilyn Monroe". Full Disclosure of CIA Involvement in the Death of Marilyn Monroe, 1988.

Zolotow, Maurice. "Joe & Marilyn: The Ultimate L.A. Love Story." *Los Angeles Times*, February 1979, pp. 138,140, 238-247.

2.   U-Tube References

[#1: U-Tube Reference]
MM's Autopsy Report 2 (1962)
https://images.app.goo.gl/PQ75s8ZFPYiJjXvc6

[#2: U-Tube Reference]
MM's Autopsy Report 1 (1962)
https://images.app.goo.gl/vbHVCGqti6ZmwiyC8

[#3: U-Tube Reference]
MM's corpse covered in blue horse blanket
https://images.app.goo.gl/v1kmRpMZ8sHjT86aA

[#4: U-Tube Reference]
The Marilyn Monroe Files [MM did not commit suicide]
https://www.youtube.com/watch?v=biYs3hR4w_8

[#5: U-Tube Reference]
MM's black raven 1956 Thunderbird sold for $490,000
https://images.app.goo.gl/cFWFzXbyWRg5RuYdA

[#6: U-Tube Reference]
MM's funeral embalmer speaks out
https://www.youtube.com/watch?v=sQf0xd2fmBQ

[#7: U-Tube Reference]
MM's Happy Birthday dress sells for: $4.81 million Nov/2016
https://www.youtube.com/watch?v=ZaCGSGekmWg

[#8: U-Tube Reference]
MM's Happy birthday dress TBA at: Julien's Auctions 17 Nov/2016
https://www.youtube.com/watch?v=hD86L-V4V_o

[#9: U-Tube Reference]
MM's home for sale for $6.9 million (SOLD for $7.25 million!)
https://www.youtube.com/watch?v=Rh2nneczS_w

[#10: U-Tube Reference]
MM: EYEWITNESS August 1962: Why?
https://www.youtube.com/watch?v=MBNIRo09aAw

[#11: U-Tube Reference]
Who Killed Marilyn Monroe? (John Miner Marilyn Transcripts 1/4)
https://www.youtube.com/watch?v=NnAhE6IADts&t=69s

[#12: U-Tube Reference]
Who Killed Marilyn Monroe? (John Miner Marilyn Transcripts 2/4)
https://www.youtube.com/watch?v=svQs0Iq6rvl&t=18s

[#13: U-Tube Reference]
Who Killed Marilyn Monroe? (John Miner Transcripts 3/4)
https://www.youtube.com/watch?v=0nF1ZN67VKY&t=6s

[#14: U-Tube Reference]
Who Killed Marilyn Monroe? (John Miner Transcripts 4/4)
https://www.youtube.com/watch?v=uQIqbzzofgM

[#15: U-Tube Reference]
Marilyn Monroe Auction - Christie's 1999 - Part 1/9
https://www.youtube.com/watch?v=YOAsqw-1scU

[#16: U-Tube Reference]
Marilyn Monroe Auction - Christie's 1999 - Part 4/9
https://www.youtube.com/watch?v=YbWD2Lt_-_4

[#17: U-Tube Reference]
Marilyn Monroe Auction - Christie's 1999 - Part 5/9
https://www.youtube.com/watch?v=4PoYbhiSKIM

[#18: U-Tube Reference]
Marilyn Monroe Auction - Christie's 1999 - Part 6/9
https://www.youtube.com/watch?v=C8uy47Hiy2A

[#19: U-Tube Reference]
MM murdered by Sam Giancana's henchmen:
[17 Feb/1992: Entertainment Tonight Exposé]
https://www.youtube.com/watch?v=3JgKlMR0PvE

[#20: U-Tube Reference]
Maf: Last dog MM had
https://images.app.goo.gl/bTenr2jozYbA8bQs8

[#21: U-Tube Reference]
Maf Honey: MM's dog
https://images.app.goo.gl/xEwA8oJjv93H8ucP9

[#22: U-Tube Reference]
Douglas Kirkland (*Look* Magazine): MM
https://www.youtube.com/watch?v=qJ44Lepus9A

[#23: U-Tube Reference]
Look Magazine with MM: Douglas Kirkland
https://www.youtube.com/watch?v=UR_eHHtv1rs

[#24: U-Tube Reference]
MM's dress for sale: Julien Auction Nov/2016 [Inside Edition]
https://www.youtube.com/watch?v=zhfQGSLoEQ0

[#25: U-Tube Reference]
MM: 10 years later (1972 Documentary)
https://www.youtube.com/watch?v=BbvmGUH3yLY

[#26: U-Tube Reference]
MM's Something's Got to Give! [8th April to 8th June 1962)]
https://www.youtube.com/watch?v=I-sLSxaaUxQ

[#27: U-Tube Reference]
MM's death: Current Affair (1 of 2)
https://www.youtube.com/watch?v=OVMzvvDHull

[#28: U-Tube Reference]
MM's Death: Current Affair (2 of 2)
https://www.youtube.com/watch?v=-I5BBkxuTpE

[#29: U-Tube Reference]
Marilyn's Suicide: Fact or Fiction? (1 of 2)
https://www.youtube.com/watch?v=YEokmJJKHpc

[#30: U-Tube Reference]
Marilyn's Suicide: Fact or Fiction? (2 of 2)
https://www.youtube.com/watch?v=AMbKIqghDYU

[#31: U-Tube Reference]
Marilyn Monroe: Suicide - Fact or Fiction? Part 1/2
https://www.youtube.com/watch?v=YEokmJJKHpc&t=20s

[#32: U-Tube Reference]
Marilyn Monroe: Suicide - Fact or Fiction? Part 2/2
https://www.youtube.com/watch?v=AMbKIqghDYU

[#33: U-Tube Reference]
Marilyn Monroe - Life After Death (1994)
https://www.youtube.com/watch?v=P-g8vUzmgNc

[#34: U-Tube Reference]
MM - Ultimate Investigation into a Suspicious Death
https://www.youtube.com/watch?v=LVyOmjWeYP0&t=155s

[#35: U-Tube Reference]
Rivals: MM vs. Jackie Kennedy (1 of 2)
https://www.youtube.com/watch?v=nQQ0X9ABXqM

[#36: U-Tube Reference]
Rivals: MM vs. Jackie Kennedy (2 of 2)
https://www.youtube.com/watch?v=X76t0SIC284

[#37: U-Tube Reference]
Jeanne Carmen & Johnny Rosselli RE: MM's death
Jeanne Carmen on Channel 9 News
https://www.youtube.com/watch?v=Rdep_Xunl_k

[#38: U-Tube Reference]
MM exhibit with Susan Strasberg: MM's 2 self-portraits
https://www.youtube.com/watch?v=Q_1qknmMaZA

[#39: U-Tube Reference]
Susan Strasberg: MM spent $5,000 on JFK b-day dress
https://www.youtube.com/watch?v=aqpDFZyUHlg

[#40: U-Tube Reference]
Susan Strasberg, Julie Miller 1988 Interview on MM
https://www.youtube.com/watch?v=MpWzOHqXp3g

[#41: U-Tube Reference]
MM: murder? Accident? Suicide?
https://www.youtube.com/watch?v=9ZeWij5QYCg

[#42: U-Tube Reference]
MM's best friend Jeanne Carmen says: MM was murdered!
https://www.youtube.com/watch?v=pt3ug9Pbg2E

[#43: U-Tube Reference]
MM's Childhood years in her own voice
https://www.youtube.com/watch?v=p34nlBUTyFM

[#44: U-Tube Reference]
MM's Teenage years in her own voice
https://www.youtube.com/watch?v=zbhS1HFwyMg

[#45: U-Tube Reference]
"After you get what you want, you don't want it!"[MM sings]
https://www.youtube.com/watch?v=pxro_JPV4sQ

[#46: U-Tube Reference]
MM's home in Brentwood SOLD 31 May 2017 for: $7.25 Million USD!
https://www.youtube.com/watch?v=LjdvqqtMNpg

[#47: U-Tube Reference]
RFK was at MM's the day she died: Dominic Dunne
https://www.youtube.com/watch?v=K-xHnBwx9nc

[#48: U-Tube Reference]
MM Christie's Auction 1999 [part one]
Total sale: $13 Million dollars to Anna Strasberg
(who never in life ever met MM!]
https://www.youtube.com/watch?v=YOAsqw-1scU

[#49: U-Tube Reference]
MM Christie's Auction 1999 [part two]
https://www.youtube.com/watch?v=UmJvpjMRpm4

[#50: U-Tube Reference]
MM Times: Theories on her death
https://www.youtube.com/watch?v=YZDsY5ltPvg

[#51: U-Tube Reference]
MM Christie's Auction 1999 [Part Eight]
https://www.youtube.com/watch?v=t9nobULLf6o

[#52: U-Tube Reference]
MM Christie's Auction 1999 [Part Nine]
https://www.youtube.com/watch?v=Qgl4crL-Sec

[#53: U-Tube Reference]
MM's Man [documentary on James Dougherty]
https://www.youtube.com/watch?v=RaCgidLF-4I

[#54: U-Tube Reference]
MM: artifacts in Ripley's Believe It or Not! museum in Hollywood
https://www.youtube.com/watch?v=Wyqtz9kmvwU

[#55: U-Tube Reference]
MM: Sussan & John Strasberg, Jane Russell, etc.
https://www.youtube.com/watch?v=oh8itsg-QPo

[#56: U-Tube Reference]
MM: Larry King Live 1997 with those who met MM
https://www.youtube.com/watch?v=TweqbfFqueA

[#57: U-Tube Reference]
MM Remembered!: Larry King Live [1st June 2001]
https://www.youtube.com/watch?v=xp0Sis5Ya5g

[#58: U-Tube Reference]
The REAL MM: John Huston, Eli Wallach, etc.
https://www.youtube.com/watch?v=NIayZlmEdjM&t=605s

[#59: U-Tube Reference]
Jeanne Carmen: MM, Frank Sinatra, JFK, RFK [start at: 20 min. mark]
https://www.youtube.com/watch?v=2QDfofFXPJg&t=1186s

[#60: U-Tube Reference]
Cal Neva Hotel history [MM there before her murder]
https://www.youtube.com/watch?v=G9xOTIei3Uc

[#61: U-Tube Reference]
Ralph Roberts, MM's Masseur: believes in foul play!
https://www.youtube.com/watch?v=xaO3vT7RIjo

[#62: U-Tube Reference]
MM and The Actor's Studio
https://www.youtube.com/watch?v=am_PvmskFnA

[#63: U-Tube Reference]
James Haspiel MM's photographer believes RFK had MM killed
https://www.youtube.com/watch?v=n5Uwrdw7mrg

[#64: U-Tube Reference]
MM's Happy Bday JFK dress SOLD: $4.81 million at Julien's Auction
https://www.youtube.com/watch?v=ZaCGSGekmWg

[#65: U-Tube Reference]
Why MM is still so closely followed in her personal effects
https://www.youtube.com/watch?v=ErVrFzjuGRw

[#66: U-Tube Reference]
MM Largest collection of memorabilia on Hotel Queen Mary
https://www.youtube.com/watch?v=yayvV_nSBWo

[#67: U-Tube Reference]
MM personal effects collected by Greg Schreiner
https://www.youtube.com/watch?v=kRmcwMhXaHg

[#68: U-Tube Reference]
MM did not commit suicide! [MM's assistant Betty Robin in 1962]
https://www.youtube.com/watch?v=wKHHv54fK_o

[#69: U-Tube Reference]
Marilyn: The Last Word [Hardcopy (30 April to 7th May 1992) into murder of MM/ 1 of 4]
https://www.youtube.com/watch?v=MXN4mMpiWyc

[#70: U-Tube Reference]
Marilyn: The Last Word [Hardcopy Investigation into the murder of MM /2 of 4]
https://www.youtube.com/watch?v=Se97xRJkLY4

[#71: U-Tube Reference]
Marilyn: The Last Word [Hardcopy Investigation into the murder of MM /3 of 4]
https://www.youtube.com/watch?v=Se97xRJkLY4

[#72: U-Tube Reference]
Marilyn: The Last Word [Hardcopy Investigation into the murder of MM /4 of 4]
Timeline of her last day on earth hour by hour
https://www.youtube.com/watch?v=5xuxgiGrkPQ

[#73: U-Tube Reference]
MM Eulogy by Lee Strasberg 8th August 1962 (at 5 min. mark)
https://www.youtube.com/watch?v=iip1w8rAz6o

[#74: U-Tube Reference]
Marilyn Monroe Auction - Christie's 1999 - Part 3/6
https://www.youtube.com/watch?v=3MQC2j9C9Is&t=33s

[#75: U-Tube Reference]
Joan Collins on Marilyn Monroe [1997]
https://www.youtube.com/watch?v=NC0t088gHgU

[#76: U-Tube Reference]
Jane Fonda on MM
https://www.youtube.com/watch?v=JMwP0hJCl4s

[#77: U-Tube Reference]
Unsolved Mysteries: MM's death
https://www.youtube.com/watch?v=9BWgjBTxwHE

[#78: U-Tube Reference]
MM's birthday dress sold for $4.81 million in 2017
https://www.youtube.com/watch?v=ZaCGSGekmWg

[#79: U-Tube Reference]
Jeanne Carmen: Second Explosive interview [Frank Sinatra, MM, JFK, RFK]
Interview at: 7 to 11-minute mark & 20-22 minute mark RE: MM murder
https://www.youtube.com/watch?v=tmTDs_0EjmQ

[#80: U-Tube Reference]
Eunice Murray, Housekeeper to MM has conflicting stories
https://www.youtube.com/watch?v=nTY-R0mZ23M

[#81: U-Tube Reference]
Robert Mitchum on MM
https://www.youtube.com/watch?v=oZKUtW-aDHM

[#82: U-Tube Reference]
Joan Collins on MM: Beware the wolves in Hollywood
https://www.youtube.com/watch?v=NC0t088gHgU

[#83: U-Tube Reference]
Shelley Winters on MM
https://www.youtube.com/watch?v=cRvwjm3eq3g

[#84: U-Tube Reference]
Laurence Olivier on MM
https://www.youtube.com/watch?v=3q995YniCsQ

[#85: U-Tube Reference]
MM's home sold for $7.25 million in 2017
https://www.youtube.com/watch?v=LjdvqqtMNpg

[#86: U-Tube Reference]
Proof Positive that MM was murdered, that RFK was there!
https://www.youtube.com/watch?v=WNVhMilngbc

[#87: U-Tube Reference]
Secret Life Story of MM
https://www.youtube.com/watch?v=u9icRUDNHHM

[#88: U-Tube Reference]
MM & Joe DiMaggio
https://www.youtube.com/watch?v=fzguiNhVd1Q

[#89: U-Tube Reference]
What Joe DiMaggio took from MM's house after her death
https://www.youtube.com/watch?v=vjoMQdPeWJU

[#90: U-Tube Reference]
The home MM died in 4th August 1962 [then & now]
https://www.youtube.com/watch?v=0PR1qR81QvA&pbjreload=10

[#91: U-Tube Reference]
MM's memorabilia SOLD and collected
https://www.youtube.com/watch?v=kRmcwMhXaHg

[#92: U-Tube Reference]
MM's home SOLD in 10 days on 31 May 2017 for $7.25 million
https://www.youtube.com/watch?v=LjdvqqtMNpg&pbjreload=10

[#93: U-Tube Reference]
"Marilyn" song sung for MM in 1952 [starts at 8-minute mark]
https://www.youtube.com/watch?v=hOGVkWRUfWI

[#94: U-Tube Reference]
Details as to why MAFIA, CIA & FBI (w/LBJ) killed: MM, JFK, & RFK
https://www.youtube.com/watch?v=0vHOcTO3rmc

[#95: U-Tube Reference]
Details of MM's embalming [so sad, so loveless]
https://www.youtube.com/watch?v=sQf0xd2fmBQ

[#96: U-Tube Reference]
Kelli Garner plays MM in "Secret Life of MM" [interview]
https://www.youtube.com/watch?v=T47RuHZledM

[#97: U-Tube Reference]
Proof that MM's doctors think they killed her [but not the whole story!]
https://www.youtube.com/watch?v=LVyOmjWeYP0

[#98: U-Tube Reference]
Anthony Summers who wrote MM biography: Goddess [1985 interview]
https://www.youtube.com/watch?v=RnxDzRxJqGc

[#99: U-Tube Reference]
How MM was murdered [see: 20-21,25-32,41-47 minute segments]
https://www.youtube.com/watch?v=TcoAEI08ms4

[#100: U-Tube Reference]
Jeanne Carmen knew that RFK was involved in MM's murder [1992 Interview]
https://www.youtube.com/watch?v=2QDfofFXPJg

[#101: U-Tube Reference]
Marilyn Monroe Party thrown at Ray Anthony's Home 1952
https://www.youtube.com/watch?v=hOGVkWRUfWI&list=RDhOGVkWRUfWI&start_radio=1

[#102: U-Tube Reference]
Ray Anthony - Marilyn
https://www.youtube.com/watch?v=cghX9sYcE9w&list=RDhOGVkWRUfWI&index=2

[#103: U-Tube Reference]
Marilyn Monroe - at the Big Band Ray Anthony Party 1952
https://www.youtube.com/watch?v=v6LO0GXCc_w&list=RDhOGVkWRUfWI&index=11

[#104: U-Tube Reference]
MM's last weekend at Cal-Neva Lodge
https://www.youtube.com/watch?v=gbyZIU09vZw

[#105: U-Tube Reference]
MM Did not commit suicide (Hard Copy)
https://www.youtube.com/watch?v=U3qgGji7UoQ

[#106: U-Tube Reference]
Double Cross - Giancana and Marilyn Monroe
https://www.youtube.com/watch?v=3JgKIMR0PvE&t=3s

[#107: U-Tube Reference]
Double Cross - Giancana and The Kennedys
https://www.youtube.com/watch?v=EGFilkbzfZ4&t=1s

[#108: U-Tube Reference]

Sam "The Cigar" Giancana's Demise

https://www.youtube.com/watch?v=c_qhgXKQKI4

[#109: U-Tube Reference]

Momo: The Sam Giancana Story

https://www.youtube.com/watch?v=obn1Y-bMk34&t=5s

[#110: U-Tube Reference]

The Mafia Murder of Marilyn Monroe [Dr. Bill Truels]

https://www.youtube.com/watch?v=0vHOcTO3rmc&t=6s

[#111: U-Tube Reference]

Jeanne Carmen - Marilyn Monroe

https://www.youtube.com/watch?v=2QDfofFXPJg&t=1491s

[#112: U-Tube Reference]

Shelley Winters on MM

https://www.youtube.com/watch?v=cRvwjm3eq3g&list=RD2QDfofFXPJg&index=9

[#113: U-Tube Reference]

Jeanne Carmen - 2nd Interview on MM

https://www.youtube.com/watch?v=tmTDs_0EjmQ&t=2s

[#114: U-Tube Reference]

Jeanne Carmen - on MM (National Inquirer)

https://www.youtube.com/watch?v=pt3ug9Pbg2E

[#115: U-Tube Reference]

Jeanne Carmen on MM [Entertainment Tonight]

https://www.youtube.com/watch?v=t1PM-SNPkQE

[#116: U-Tube Reference]

Jeanne Carmen on MM [History Buff]

https://www.youtube.com/watch?v=KfcBarDpOel

[#117: U-Tube Reference]

Jeanne Carmen on MM [Channel 9 News]

https://www.youtube.com/watch?v=Rdep_Xunl_k

[#118: U-Tube Reference]

The Marilyn Monroe Files

https://www.youtube.com/watch?v=biYs3hR4w_8&t=2541s

[#119: U-Tube Reference]

MM interviewed by George Belmont for Marie Claire Magazine [April 1966]

https://www.youtube.com/watch?v=3wfMzdlMA00

[#120: U-Tube Reference]

MM sings: "Specialization!"

https://www.youtube.com/watch?v=FLhTrjQU8Pk

[#120: U-Tube Reference]

After you get what you want, you don't want it! [Marilyn Monroe sings]

https://www.youtube.com/watch?v=jlooRreqEt4&list=RDMM&index=25

[#122: U-Tube Reference]

Leonard Cohen: Take This Longing [with Lyrics]

https://www.youtube.com/watch?v=Y2cafzCEokk

3. *Wikipedia* References

The references in Wikipedia that I consulted in the course of this research include the following: (1) John F. Kennedy; (2) Robert F. Kennedy; (3) Margot Patricia Newcomb; (4) Ethel Kennedy; (5) Sam Giancana; (6) Johnny Rosselli; (7) Thomas Nigochi; (8) Theodore Curphy; (9) Lionel Grandison; (10) John Miner; (11) Ralph Greenson; (12) Hymen Engelby; (13) Lee Strasberg; (14) Susan Strasberg; (15) John Strasberg; (16) Anna Strasberg; (17) Paula Strasberg; (18) Laurence Olivier; (19) Jane Russell; (20) Jeanne Carmen; (21) J. Edgar Hoover; (22) Eunice Murray; (23) Norman Jeffries; (24) George Barris; (25) Richard Meryman; (26) (Laurence) Larry Schiller; (27) Robert Mitchum; (28) Daryll Zanuck; (29) William Parker; (30) Mickey Rooney; (31) Arthur Miller; (32) Arthur Jacobs; (33) Natalie Trundy; (34) Johnny Hyde; (35) Milton Berle; (36) Hope Lange; (37) Robert Wagner; (38) James Hospiel; (39) David Brower; (40) Donald O'Connel; (41) Jack Clemmons; (42) Tony Curis; (43) Ralph Roberts; (44) Joe DiMaggio, Sr.; (45) Joe DiMaggio, Jr.; (46) Peter Lawford; (47) Dean Martin; (48) Cyd Charisse; (49) Milton Greene; (50) Amy Greene; (51) James Dougherty; (52) Bob Slatzer; (53) Bernie Spindel; (54) Jimmy Hoffa; (55) Milo Sperighio; (56) Kirk Douglas; (57) Frank Sinatra; (58) Joey Bishop; (59) Sammy Davis, Jr.; (60) James Bacon; (61) Anthony Summers; (62) Betty Robin; (63) Carl Sandburg; (64) Judith Exner; (65) Berniece Baker Miracle; (66) Clark Gable; (67) Montgomery Clift; (68) Eli Wallach; (69) Dean Hall; (70) George Carpozi; (71) Mickey Rudin; (72) Leonard "Needles"

Gianola (b.19 Nov/1910); (73) James "Mugsy" Tortorella; (74) Charles Stanley Gifford; (75) William Boewan; (76) Phyllis McGuire; (77) Dan Stewart; (78) Natalie Jacobs; (79) Karl Menninger; (80) Norman Mailer; (81) Henry Weinstock; (82) Hedda Hopper; (83) Elia Kazan; (84) Robert Blakely; (85) Marilyn Monroe; (86) Frank Shuran; (87) Tony Promanzano; (88) Charles "Chuckie" O'Brian; (89) Donovan Wells; (90) Dave Beck; (91) Bob Meryhew; (92) Lee Harvey Oswald; (93) Jack Rubenstein "Ruby"; (94) Frank Lazono; (95) Carlos Marcello; (96) Ed Partner; (97) Judith Cambell Exner; (98) Bay of Pig Fiasco (17 April 1961); (99) Cuban Missile Crisis (Oct/1962); (100) Richard Cane; (101) Murray Humphreys; (102) Tony Ricardo; (103) Paul Ricardo; (104) "Always in my Heart"; (105) Chukie English; (106) Butch Glaney; (107) Chukie Nicolletti; (108) Milwauke Phil; (109) Al Durisso; (110) Pepe Giancana; (111) J.D. Tippett; (112) Oscar White; (113) Leonard Nimoy; (114) Bernard Spindell; (115) Emma J. Atchison (1867-1921); (116) Grace Goddard; (117) Marvin Runyou; (118) Doris Howell; (119) Jeff Howell; (120) Elvis Presley; (121) Marlon Brando; (122) Otis Monroe; (123) Della Monroe; (124) Jacob Monroe; (125) Mary Monroe; (126) Fiford Hogan; (127) Jena Hogan; (128) Robert Litman; (129) Jack Benny; (130) Donald H. Wolfe; (131) Cyril Wecht; (132) Robert Forrest; (133) Michael Selsman; (134) Hugh Hefner; (135) Leonard Cohen; (136) Elizabeth Taylor; (137) Joseph L. Mankiewicz; (138) George Cukor; (139) Spyros P. Skouras; (140) Eddie Jones; (141) Joe Margolis; (142) Tim Purtell; (143) Alan Synder; (144) Bert Stern; (145) Greg Schreiner; and so forth.

[Many more researched but not noted in my records: my apologies!]

Part Five: To Lie, or Not to Lie?

A.   Walking in a Minefield of Lies

1.   Social Cement v. "Reign of Terror"

Hamlet asks the existential question: "To be, or not to be" (Hamlet, Act III, scene 1) wondering whether it is better to live or to die in battle. Today, we affirm: "To lie, or not to lie? That is the Question!". Even the "Big Lies" of today appear to reach little or no resolution. We feel at times that we are not casually 'tiptoeing through the tulips' as in a time of peace.

But instead we can sense the tremors of turmoil as Truth becomes the 'first casualty' in this minefield of lies that beset us (virtually on every side). All too often we are witnessing the decline and even pending collapse of public trust.

This 'social cement' (that 'invisible bond that binds people together', that unites communities, that gives us a feeling of identity, as a group, or as a society) is now sorely needed. In 1789, in Paris, when that 'social cement' finally came apart, the result was devastating: The guillotine was used in the literal beheading of thousands of people in the ruling class. This total collapse of public trust in the French Government was dubbed: "The Reign of Terror.'

2.   Big Brother's "Noble Lie"

Leaders of a future World Government today do not wish a repeat of history, of 1789 France. Indeed, they look for ways to keep the crowds in check, even if it is to offer them free 'bread and circus' as the ancient Romans did when their civilization declined and eventually collapsed. But these endless social programs may not be enough.

Plato envisioned an ideal society that was based upon "noble lies" (*The Republic*, Book III, 414), lies that were not only for the elite groups, the Guardians, the ruling class of Gold, but for the lower classes of Silver and Brass, as well. This concept of the "noble lie" was a type of 'pious fiction', a contradictory term much like the 'doublethink' reality-control language used by Big Brother (in Orwell's *1984*).

Both concepts sought the same goal: To maintain social harmony, or to advance their own (private) agenda.

3.   'Sweet Lies' of a (Russian) Police State

As the war drums of the past sound louder and louder, we see the result of the Russian Regime in East Europe (and elsewhere). They wish to advance their own agenda.

For their propaganda machine of 'sweet lies' reassures their populace and other people partial to their *'putsch'* into Ukraine, for example, that there is 'no war', that there is 'no invasion' across their neighbor's border. There is no intention to overthrow the peaceful Government of Kyiv, they want all of us to believe.

For Ukrainians are 'little Russians' who naturally bond and belong to Mother Russia, as one people. Putin said as much in his 5,000-word essay written last July (2021). So, it must be true. Every Russian can believe these 'sweet lies'. That is their duty, to conform to the dictates of the 'Great Dictator,' who naturally knows what is best for everyone.

And so, as if they were all mere mass victims of the Stockholm Syndrome, the captives of these 'sweet lies' actually develop positive feelings towards their captors, over time. And so, even Big Lies continue to be spread repeatedly. (Why settle for just 'little lies' when the people appear so gullible?!)

For that is the essence of the Authoritarian Regime: to follow the 4 D's 'religiously.'

(a) Firstly, to DENY that there are any war crimes, any atrocities, or anything amiss in their occupied territories (whether at home or abroad).
(b) Secondly, to DELAY any national or international inquiry into these 'alleged' wrong doings.
(c) Thirdly, to DENOUNCE the opposing side to have committed the identical crimes (of which the Regime is accused), to transfer the blame to the other side, those victimized by the Regime.
(d) And, fourthly, to DESTROY all incriminating evidence, to rewrite the history of the events that occurred, as it were.

In so doing, and following these 4 steps, the security of the Police State is reassured. For 'National Security' is the ultimate justification for each and every necessary action, regardless of what it might be.

B.   What Does the Future Hold?

1.   The Brotherhood: An Organized Revolt

In Orwell's *1984*, the future appears quite bleak. People want to have a good time, but The Party (ruling elites) want to stop you. So, you break the rules as best as you can, but try to keep alive. It is all that simple (according to Julia, Winston's secret lover).

But Winston sees the future of the younger generation (differently): Not as a people who would form a Brotherhood, an organized revolt, against the Party, but as "people who had grown up in the world of the Revolution, knowing nothing else, accepting the Party as something unalterable, like the sky, not rebelling against its authority but simply evading it, as a rabbit dodges a dog" (*1984*, p.108).

2.   Our Future: As Bright as Our Faith

As we consider the future, especially for this younger generation, we see that there is a consistency in believing that with a positive view, positive results may occur. The future it appears is only 'as bright as our faith.'

In the Scriptures, we are reminded that we ought not to be deceived as "God is not mocked: for whatsoever a man soweth, that shall he also reap" (Galatians 6:7). This phenomenon can be also conceived as 'the butterfly effect'. Simply put, the 'butterfly effect' is 'a phenomenon whereby a tiny change (as in the flapping of the wings of a butterfly) can carry large repercussions over time.'

The philosopher William James makes this case: That everything we do for good or ill will have a permanent inalterable effect, as follows:

> We are spinning our own fates, good or evil, never to be undone. Every stroke of virtue or vice leaves its ever-little scar. The drunken Rip Van Winkle, in Jefferson's play, excuses himself for every fresh dereliction by saying: "I won't count this time!".

> Well, he may not count it, and a kind Heaven may not count it; but it's being counted none the less. Down among his nerve-cells and fibers, *the molecules are counting it* (!), registering and storing it up to be used against him when the *next* temptation comes.

> *Nothing* we ever do is, in strict literalness, wiped out!

3.   To Re-learn Past Lessons

Paul, the Apostle of 2,000 years ago, held a stern reminder for all believers when he said: "We wrestle not against flesh and blood, but against principalities, against powers, against the rulers of the darkness of this world, against spiritual wickedness in high places" (Ephesians 6:12).

Perhaps we would do well to heed Paul's insight as it appears equally applicable in our day.

As a more recent ballad (from 1960) relates:

> Where have all the flowers gone?
> Young girls have picked them everyone!
>
> Where have all the young girls gone?
> Gone for husbands everyone!
>
> Where have all the husbands gone?
> Gone for soldiers everyone!
>
> Where have all the soldiers gone?
> Gone to graveyards everyone!
>
> Where have all the graveyards gone?
> Gone to flowers everyone.
>
> Oh, *when* will they ever learn?

[see, the U-Tube Reference below:]

Where Have All the Flowers Gone? (Kingston Trio)
https://www.youtube.com/watch?v=9hxg3B-1OsA